"SIWANATORZ ARE STRONG, CONFIDENT, AND BELIEVE IN THEMSELVES AND OTHERS"

—JoJo Siwa XOXO

# JoJo's GUIDE TO THE Sweet Life

## #PeaceOutHaterz

BY JOJO SIWA

Cataloging-in-Publication Data has been applied for
and may be obtained from the Library of Congress.

ISBN 978-1-4197-2817-4

Pages ii–iii, x, 2, 17, 88, 200: photos copyright © CBI Distributing Corp.
Pages 46, 74, 100, 108, 116, 140, 150, 166, 182, 229:
photos copyright © BluBot Studios.
Page 152: photo courtesy Matt Yoakum (@mattslayss).
All other photos permission of Jessalynn Siwa.

Text copyright © 2017 JoJo Siwa
Jacket and title page illustrations copyright © 2017 Amulet Books
Book design by Timothy Shaner / Night and Day Design

Printed and bound in USA

10 9 8 7 6 5

Amulet Books are available at special discounts when purchased in
quantity for premiums and promotions as well as fundraising or
educational use. Special editions can also be created to specification.
For details, contact specialsales@abramsbooks.com or the address below.

ABRAMS The Art of Books
195 Broadway, New York, NY 10007
abramsbooks.com

For everyone who
believed in me;
and if you're
reading this,
I believe in you!

# CONTENTS

# 1

# Rolo-s for Being A Siwanator

#SiwanatorzRule

# HI, EVERYONE!
# I'M JOJO SIWA,
## AND THIS IS MY STORY.

**I GREW UP IN OMAHA, NEBRASKA,** where my mom owned a dance studio. I had an incredible, supportive family and all my friends beside me. My childhood was the best time—yet I always knew what my future was going to be. You see, from the time I was really little, I wanted to be a pop star. Now I'm lucky enough to be living out my dreams.

In a minute I'm going to tell you how it all began—from my first solo at age two, all the way through the amazing things I'm doing right now. But first I want to talk about what it is to be a Siwanator. I'm guessing if you picked up this book, you're probably a Siwanator already! Or maybe you've seen my hit single, "Boomerang," on YouTube . . . but you're not totally sure what it means to be a Siwanator.

Siwanatorz are the backbone of this book. Being a Siwanator means being confident, positive, and supportive of others. Sometimes it means building a wall around you—and I'm not talking

about the kind you make with bricks. I'm talking about the imaginary kind that keeps the haters away. When someone is hating, you just imagine that wall around you, protecting you. Think, "I can't hear you, I can't see you . . . what you're saying just doesn't matter!" Then go find the people who love you for who you are, and hang with them instead. They're the ones who really count!

Siwanatorz protect each other. If they see someone being bullied, they speak up. Maybe not to the bully herself—but to a parent or teacher.

And even more important, they are kind to the person who is being bullied. A little kindness can go a long way . . . I've seen it firsthand. Let me tell you a story from when I was in third grade. It stuck with me for life, because it was one of the first times I saw someone being bullied and decided to do something about it.

My whole life, I've been homeschooled, except for kindergarten and one quarter in third grade. When I was in third grade, I went back to school for the last quarter of the year to see what it was like and to make sure I was on track. (I was! I scored off the charts on my NESA test and had a lot of fun making new friends; but in the end I decided I liked being homeschooled better.) The first day I got to school in the third grade, the other girls came up to me and pointed out another girl in the class. They said, "We don't like her. You're not going to hang out with her because we don't."

At first I just kind of went along with it. I didn't know what to do—I was just the new kid. It was a nice school in a nice neighborhood, and if you didn't have the "right" clothes or were a little different, it was harder to fit in. The popular girls were really mean to this other girl, who I'm going to call Lucy. (That's not her real name.) That semester, we were learning our multiplication facts, and Lucy was behind. We learned all the way up through 12—and each time we got a whole set of numbers right, we got to build an ice cream sundae on a chart on the wall. At the end of the year, there was going to be an ice cream party where we got real sundaes! So if you got all your 1's right (1x1, 1x2, 1x3, and on), you got a bowl. Then if you got all your 2's right (2x1, 2x2, 2x3, and on), you got whipped cream. It went like that, all the way up to 12, and there were all kinds of toppings: cherries, bananas, Oreos, everything you could want! At 12's, you got your scoop of ice cream.

Finally the end of the year arrived, and everyone was having the party. We were all in the cafeteria with our bowls filled with ice cream and toppings, having fun . . . except for Lucy. She was sitting in the corner crying. She had only gotten through her 2's, so she only had a bowl with whipped cream. No other toppings. Not even ice cream.

Lucy had her hands over her face, crying, all alone. It was terrible. Something clicked inside me—this wasn't okay, and it wasn't gonna happen on my watch. So I got up from where I was sitting with my friends, got another round of ice cream with all

the toppings, and took it over to Lucy. I made the best sundae I could think of, then sat next to her while she ate it. I saw how happy it made her. And I regretted not playing with her at recess that year, not inviting her to my house. After I sat next to Lucy, all the other kids came and sat with us and started talking to her. All I had to do was make the first move.

What happened with Lucy always stuck with me. I like to tell kids now, "Just be nice! You'll regret it when you're older if you don't."

I'm constantly reminded of that day with Lucy, every time I see anyone else who doesn't fit in. It makes me think, "I wish I would have done something." But then I remember: In the end, I did. In the end, we were friends.

Now I'd tell someone like Lucy, "Don't let them bother you. When someone is yelling at you or ignoring you, it's never about what it seems." That person who's calling you ugly or stupid? Maybe they're getting told they're ugly. Usually anger comes from pain—a lot of times bullies have been hurt themselves, and their way of dealing with it is to lash out. Remembering this helps me be kind to everyone, even the bullies. No one is perfect, so the only thing we can all do is just be ourselves and trust that we'll find our real friends. That's why I created Siwanatorz!

Siwanatorz are the whole rainbow, and proud of it! We're from all over the world. We're all types of people. We're silly and quirky and fun and accepting and *kind*. And most of all, we hold each other up for being individuals. We're all unique!

Being a Siwanator is about feeling good about yourself . . . and that means every part of you. I'm constantly thinking of ways for

# BEING A SIWANATOR IS ABOUT FEELING GOOD ABOUT YOURSELF... AND THAT MEANS EVERY PART OF YOU!

us all to be different together. For all of us to celebrate the parts of ourselves that might be a little weird and a little crazy . . . and a lot AWESOME!

Once I challenged #Siwanatorz to show the world they weren't afraid to do something wild: →

I wondered if anyone would actually do it. And guess what? You did.

*Thousands of you!*

Turns out, there are a lot of wild, fun, hilarious Siwanatorz out there who aren't afraid to be different! And together, we are even stronger.

**itsjojosiwa** Siwanator Sunday 🎀🎀🎀 siwanators are strong, confident and awesome !! **#peaceouthaterz** mismatched socks this week because it's fun to be different 🖤🤍🤍🖤🖤 post your mismatched socks to **#peaceouthaterz**

Together, no one can stop us! When you're feeling low, or if you need extra support—tweet at me with #siwanatorz. If you're a Siwanator, you're never alone. Even if I can't respond personally, the community we've created together is there for you.

Siwanatorz always have each other's backs, no matter what!

# JoJo's Guide to Being a Siwanator

# Be positive!

Be confident and kind. Believe in yourself and others. Be encouraging, and shake off negativity. MOST OF ALL, BE NICE TO OTHERS. Whether it's opening a door for someone or telling them you like their outfit, always be encouraging and positive to other people. Not too long ago, I was tagged in an online post. A girl was the winner of her classroom spelling bee, and she was nervous about going on to the next level. She was even thinking about dropping out of the competition! Then her mom reminded her that Siwanatorz are confident! And she told her to put on her favorite bow and go out there and do her best. So what did that girl do? She channeled all her confidence, handed her mom the hairbrush, and asked for a side ponytail topped with a big bow! Then she walked onto that spelling bee stage with confidence, and even made it to the top ten.

Hearing that story felt so good—it reminded me we can all make a difference, even in someone's day-to-day. We're all there for each other! So don't forget to say and do nice things—*especially* when someone's having a hard time.

It's also important to stay positive in your own mind! Tell yourself, "Today's going to be a great day!" Find something good to focus on, even if it's just that you're wearing your favorite pair of pants. Siwanatorz are kind to others and also confident in themselves—so be proud of who you are, and be happy!

## Stand up to bullies.

This is a big thing Siwanatorz do. If there's a bully, stand up to them! There are two ways to stand up to bullies: bully them back, or tell them politely what they're doing wrong. The second one is what Siwanatorz do. A Siwanator would go up to a bully and say, "You shouldn't be doing this—it's wrong." Then a Siwanator would invite the person being bullied over—because that's going to make their day! It's easy to go up to someone and say, "Hey, what's wrong? Come hang out with me!"

Sometimes bullies will keep being mean even after you ask them to stop. In that case, it's really important to tell an adult. Bullying that goes on for a long time can be really hurtful and damaging. An adult you trust—a parent, teacher, or counselor—will know what to do to make it stop and how to get help for the person who was bullied.

"Hey, what's wrong?
Come hang out
with me!"

It can be scary to speak up, but be brave! Helping someone else is always the right thing to do.

Remember, nice is awesome. It's not about being the most popular kid in school or having the best clothes. It's about being happy with who you are and how you treat other people. If you're not the coolest kid in school, don't worry about it! If you're happy, it's going to be a great life.

## Wear something fun and different.

Or just wear something fun that represents *you*. Siwanatorz aren't afraid to be a little different. So if everyone's

wearing sweatpants, we wear sequins! Don't feel like you need to look like everyone else to fit in! Don't even worry about fitting in at all—just be yourself. I see myself as a transplanted eighties girl—so that's how I dress! Maybe you want to wear a cape. Or a tutu! Just do it—be your wacky, wonderful self! Less is not more.

## Make your own rules!

The beauty of being a Siwanator is that we're inclusive! Is there something that means a lot to you, which you think should be included in the Siwanator rulebook? Tweet it at me using #SiwanatorRulez.

## Follow your dreams!

No matter what, always follow your passions! Doing the things you love can help take your mind off bullying, or other hurtful problems. And best of all, it can help you find great friends. So if you're into ice-skating, join a team! Or if you're into board games and there isn't already a club, start one! Putting your energy into things that make you happy will remind you of what's most important—staying true to yourself. Best of all, bullies can't take that away!

EVEN THEN,
I KNEW...
BOWS
ARE "MY
SUPERPOWER"

—JoJo Siwa XOXO

# What's YOUR Superpower?

# 2

# Sugar Babies

# ALL THE BIG KIDS LOVED HELPING ME OUT WITH DANCING, AND I HAVE A MILLION AMAZING MEMORIES.

**I HAVE ALWAYS LOVED DANCING.** From the time my brother and I were babies, my mom's studio, Dance Unlimited, was my second home. My mom says that even when I was just a year and a half old, I'd sit in the corner, taking it all in. I loved it. I remember hanging out with the big girls at the studio—playing hide-and-seek with them and playing in the snow. It was so much fun—the best childhood. There was never a time when I didn't want to hang out over there.

One of the best parts of being at my mom's studio all the time was watching the girls prepare for their competitions. I loved everything about it: the wooden floors, the crazy dressing rooms, the beautiful costumes, and the music they played for each new routine! But most of all, I loved the students. I'd watch them practice for hours before, studying their choreography.

My older brother is the all-time best; but growing up, I had dozens of big sisters at the studio. They were always playing with me, braiding my hair and sneaking me pieces of candy.

# What does your FAVORITE CANDY say about YOU?

## RAZZLE DAZZLE
You love to laugh and have a great time with friends—you're the center of attention!

## REESE'S PIECES
You know what you like, and you stick with it. You're a loyal friend who inspires trust!

## SWEETARTS
You're a summer kind of kid—you love being outside, soaking up the sun. You're radiant!

## ALMOND JOY
You're a little quirky, and proud of it! You're a leader and stand out from the pack.

## MILK DUDS
You're patient and kind. You're the one in your group everyone turns to for advice!

(You guys know that's the quickest way to my heart!) I've never felt bad that I don't have any real sisters, because there were so many awesome girls to hang out with at dance. The only thing I *didn't* like was being constantly touched! Since I was the cute little kid, they all wanted to touch my hair and hug me all the time. Even now, I'm not that touchy-feely!

All the big kids loved helping me out with dancing, and I have a million amazing memories from those early years. Even at 6 A.M. in the freezing-cold Nebraska winters, I'd beg my mom to take me along to competitions.

I WAS ALWAYS AN OUTGOING, CONFIDENT KID. SOMETIMES WHEN I WAS A TODDLER AND MY PARENTS HAD PEOPLE OVER, I'D HOP OUT OF BED AT MIDNIGHT TO DANCE FOR THEM.

When I was two, I danced onstage in a diaper—I was a baby ant dancing on top of a giant peanut butter and jelly sandwich! It was one of my very first competitions! Other times when I tagged along with my mom to competitions, I'd make my own random fun. My mom would be really busy helping the other girls with their costumes, hair, and makeup and organizing their dances. One time when she went looking for me after she was done, she found me

in the back of a nacho stand! I'd asked the vendors if I could help—I'd been making nachos all day! I always found ways to entertain myself while my mom was working. Sometimes I just ran around collecting the rhinestones that fell off other girls' costumes.

One day my mom and I went to Cold Stone Creamery for some ice cream. We were standing in line when the guy behind the counter said, "Hi, JoJo!" My mom was so confused about how I knew the Cold Stone guy. It turned out

he was one of my competition friends—I'd helped him out at the music hall ice cream stand a few months before!

I was always an outgoing, confident kid. Sometimes when I was a toddler and my parents had people over, I'd hop out of bed at midnight to dance for them, then go right back to bed once I'd finished. I was never really a baby—or at least I didn't act like one. I ordered my own food in restaurants, even when I was as little as four. One of my family's favorite Little JoJo stories is when, around the time I was three years old, I was sitting outside in my stroller and my mom—who is the best mom ever—hadn't dressed me warmly enough. It got really, really cold in Nebraska! So that particular day, I leaned out of my stroller and twisted around and said, "You should have dressed me better, Mom!" We laugh about that all the time. My mom never babied us, though, and that time was no exception. She just said, "You're fine," and that was that.

Because I had such a strong personality at such a young age, it was no surprise to anyone that I was determined to dance from the time I could walk.

I was that girl who ran across the grass in a tutu, or cartwheeled down the grocery aisle. At home, my parents always knew where to find me: in our basement, making up dances to my favorite songs. When I was little, I wanted to be dancing *all the time*. Lucky for me, there were plenty of chances.

Sure, I was a toddler. But I was a toddler with confidence. I wasn't about to let something as insignificant as age stop me. (Age has never stopped me, even now!) As I got older, I wanted to be more and more like the older dancers.

# What are your FAVORITE SONGS to dance to?

List them below!

# What do you LOVE to do more than anything else?

Check the box next to all that apply, and add your own!

❏ Eat ice cream

❏ Paint

❏ Hang with your friends

❏ Act out a play

❏ Sing karaoke

❏ Read comic books

❏ Play video games

❏ Swim

❏ . . . . . . . . . . . . . . . . . . . . . . . . . .

❏ . . . . . . . . . . . . . . . . . . . . . . . . . .

❏ . . . . . . . . . . . . . . . . . . . . . . . . . .

❏ . . . . . . . . . . . . . . . . . . . . . . . . . .

I was a total beginner back then, but determination has always been my strong suit. I was never intimidated by the other dancers, no matter how amazing they were. I spun it into a positive—I had a chance to learn and push myself! I honestly can't remember a time when I was afraid to give something a try. Here's the thing, though: I might have been born dancing, but no one's born a dancer—it takes years of work to get there. I didn't even know what that word *plié* meant until I was a few years older.

I practiced all day long when I was little. When my mom was in the kitchen getting stuff ready for dinner, she'd turn the music on, and I'd hang out and do my routines while she ordered pizza. My mom has always been so amazing! If she ever got sick of my endless practice, she never once let on. And I clearly never got sick of it myself.

I figured this out way later: When you have a passion for something, it mostly doesn't feel like work. I wanted so badly to be on that stage, and eventually my mom gave in. She saw what was obvious: I may have just barely learned to walk, but I was meant to perform. That's how I finally got . . . *drumroll* . . . my very first solo! I'd been waiting my whole life (two whole years) for this opportunity. I was entered in the "Musical Theater Four and Under" division. For my number, my mom picked a song from *Hairspray* called "Mama I'm a Big Girl Now." How perfect was that? The lyrics in the song talk about a child aged two, just like I was.

That day at *Kids Artistic Revue*, where I danced my first solo, my dream was about to come true! And, funny thing, I wasn't nervous at all. That was good, since everyone else seemed nervous enough *for* me! People were so worried I'd forget the choreography or freak out when the lights came up and I saw all the people in the audience staring. They kept asking me questions: How was I feeling—did I need anything? Was I excited?

I wasn't worried. If I had one concern,
it was maybe makeup—I hated it!

As for my costume, I would have slept in it if I could! I've always loved dressing up, and my mom got a special outfit made for my solo. One of the best things about being a dancer? You don't have to wait for Halloween to wear costumes. And this one was especially great: a pink top covered in rhinestones and a fluffy orange skirt that bounced when I moved. My mom curled my hair and put it in two pigtails that were adorable puffs on the top of my head.

ONE OF THE BEST THINGS ABOUT BEING A DANCER? YOU DON'T HAVE TO WAIT FOR HALLOWEEN TO WEAR COSTUMES...

My favorite part? The huge, glittery orange bows! (As many of you know, my bows have stuck with me over the years—they're now my signature thing!)

Once I had on my makeup and costume, I was ready . . . I just had to wait! My mom says I was practically hopping up and down with excitement. "Is it my turn?" I kept asking her.

"Not yet," she said. I was so ready! From the side of the stage, I couldn't see the audience, but I could see the girl performing before me. I watched her finish up her solo. In just a few seconds, that would be me! My mom did a last-minute check, making sure everything was ready. Next to her, my prop—a big pink box, with orange flowers (it matched my costume!)—was waiting. On it was a smiley face my mom had drawn so I'd know where to put my hand during my routine. My mom reached down to get the box, and I took that second to peek between the curtains. That's when I saw . . .

Hundreds of faces! Friends, students, parents, brothers, sisters, competitors . . . all staring out from the darkness. I probably should have been scared out of my mind, but I wasn't—I couldn't wait!

Finally they announced my category and the name of my routine: "Baby Diva"! Could anything have been more perfect? Immediately, the audience started clapping and cheering. Some even shouted "Go JoJo!" (We have it all on tape!)

Finally I was doing it! I was dancing onstage for a real audience!

"Mama, I gotta tell you without a doubt," the song went, and I'd lift my hands and shimmy, "I get my best dancing lessons from you!"Crazy, right? I was still wearing diapers—that's how little I was!

I wanted it to go on and on forever. But before I knew it, I was taking my place back on the box for the final verse of the song. A few more steps, the last line . . . and I took my final pose just a little early—I folded my arms and leaned on the box. It wasn't even part of the routine!

The singer let loose the final line: "Mama, I'm a big girl now!"

The audience exploded!

I was so happy. I held the pose for a second; then I jumped off the box and bolted off the stage to find my mom and my friends. I knew I'd done a great job.

## I also knew I was exactly where I was meant to be.

Check out the vid yourselves! It's on my YouTube channel: https://www.youtube.com/watch?v=yLA7bhRrpFs

Leave me a comment with #JoJosGuide below the video!

# JoJo's Guide to Being Center Stage

# Practice! Practice always makes perfect.

When I was little, I used to practice twenty-five hours of dance per week, because it was my favorite thing and I always wanted to get better. I loved going into my basement and rehearsing and practicing my turns. Sometimes it's hard to practice—sometimes you'd rather watch TV or play video games! But if you want to get better, it takes hard work!

# Know what's right for you.

If you're playing softball and it's not your favorite thing in the world, don't be afraid to try something new. You have to understand and know what you love. Maybe your passion is acting, or drawing! Maybe you dance like I do, or maybe you play the violin, or recite poetry, or figure skate. Or maybe you're a really good friend, the one everyone comes to when they have a problem. Think all the time about what makes you happy. First, though, give yourself the space to try out a bunch of different things—there's no need to figure it all out right away. I tried softball and it was fun; but eventually during fast-pitch softball, I was afraid of the speed of the ball, so I went back to dancing. Never be afraid to try new things! You've gotta know what works for you.

## Never give up.

If you're doing something you love, and you want to continue doing it in your future, don't give up! Sometimes it can be hard. Sometimes you might want to quit. But always remember that you love doing it, and that it makes you happy. With anything you do there will always be highs and lows. If you're a dancer, one day maybe you're the best, and the next day you might be the worst. But you always have to work your hardest and never give up.

It's okay not to be the best! It's about loving what you do. When I was little, my mom always told me it's not about the win. It's about being happy! I'm happiest when I've worked really hard to reach my goals. If I try my absolute best and enjoy what I'm doing, nothing else matters— definitely not what a panel of judges thinks!

## Know how to say, "Thank you."

It's very important, when someone gives you a compliment, to always say thank you. My mom taught me when I was little never to say "thanks." She taught me to look a person in the eye and say, "Thank you!" Genuinely appreciate the compliment and don't contradict it. As my mom always tells me, "Don't dumb yourself down." Sometimes someone will say something nice and you might want to say, "Well, it wasn't my best." But why say that? If they're taking the time to give you a compliment, they most likely mean it—so own it!

What makes you HAPPIEST?
List five things that
make you SPARKLE!

# Know when it's your time to shine.

No matter what happens in your life, you will come across an opportunity to show everyone what you can do. So wait your turn. When someone else is dancing, make sure you're clapping! The more you compete—and the better you get— you'll realize that no one wins *all the time*. Eventually it's going to be your time to shine, and you'll want other people to cheer *you* on. When someone's doing something really cool, be happy for them. Then when it's your turn, love every moment of it. My mom and I always say, "Life is like an upside-down pyramid—there's room for everyone at the top." When other girls have won competitions instead of me, I've gone right over and congratulated them. I'll give them a hug, because that's what I'd want each of them to do if I'd won. Wanting others to have success is part of being a Siwanator too. We can all have our moment in the spotlight!

# Believe in yourself.

If you want to do well and you want to be successful, know it all comes from you: your heart and your mind. You have to believe in yourself. If you believe, "I'm gonna go out on

# Create your own MANTRA!

Fill in the blank with something you are.
(For example: I am powerful!)

I am . . . . . . . . . . . . . . . . . . . . . . . . . . . !

I am . . . . . . . . . . . . . . . . . . . . . . . . . . . !

I am . . . . . . . . . . . . . . . . . . . . . . . . . . . !

When you're feeling low, do the same thing—close your eyes and remind yourself of all the things that make you the amazing person you are. Remember: *Siwanatorz are strong, confident, and powerful*!

Be . . . . . . . . . . . . . . . . . . . . . . . . . . . !
(For example: happy/bubbly/excited/creative)

Be . . . . . . . . . . . . . . . . . . . . . . . . . . . !
(For example: sweet/friendly/fun/silly)

Be YOU!

the baseball field and catch the ball and be amazing," you'll do it! But if your confidence is low and you're thinking, "I'm nervous for today," it'll be harder. Just be ready! Be ready to catch the ball, or to dance! When people ask me what my best advice is, I say, "Believe in yourself!" Whenever I'm feeling down, I tell myself, "My name is JoJo Siwa. I've got this."

I'll tell you my experiences and stories in these pages, but this is also a place for you to put your own hopes and dreams—to remember what makes you the most fun, kindest, most confident girl around!

Always follow your dreams, Siwanatorz! Even when it gets tough, it's worth it. And don't be afraid to tell the world what you love and just how special you are!

# 3

# My Peeps

#FamilyMatters

# MY PARENTS WERE ALL ABOUT FAMILY VALUES AND MAKING SURE WE STAY GROUNDED.

**GROWING UP WITH MY FAMILY** in Nebraska was great. My childhood was so much fun—my brother and I used to swim in the backyard morning, noon, and night. We grew up eating popsicles and grilling out and playing with Super Soakers. There was never any fighting, because we just knew to respect each other. My parents were all about family values and making sure we stayed grounded, and all of us always spent a lot of time together. My brother even did hip-hop dance at my mom's studio when he was five!

People tell me all the time how lucky I am, and I agree 100 percent. It's just the four of us: me, my mom (Jessalynn), my dad (Tom), and my brother (Jayden). Plus all our dogs! We're extremely close—all best friends.

# Family TRIVIA!

Ask your family the following questions, and have everyone write their answers on pieces of paper. Then fold up the papers and shuffle them all around in a box. Take turns pulling answers, and guessing whose they are!

- What's your first memory?
- Who in the family do you look the most like?
- What's your favorite dessert?
- What's your favorite sports team?
- What's the third letter of your middle name?
- What celebrity would play you in a movie?
- What's your favorite memory from a family vacation?

The boys—that's what I call my dad and my brother—live in Nebraska, and the girls live in California, now that my career has taken off. We have an amazing family, and just really balance each other out. I love going back to Omaha to visit the boys, though of course I can't wait until they move out to Los Angeles and we're all together again after Jayden graduates from high school. (He wants to go to college in California!)

But for now, we make it work—because that's what family does, and we're really supportive of one another.

I have different relationships with everyone in my family. My mom and I are *so* close. We go really well together, because our personalities are complementary—she's more chill than I am, and I'm the bubbly one. It's pretty much perfect. My mom has always been my number one biggest supporter. She's always been the driving force of this train. I was never forced to dance, or to do anything I've done over the years—but if I wanted it, my mom was right there encouraging and investing her time and energy into it.

My mom is with me every single day of my life. We've been through thick and thin, and we're basically best friends. Our code names for each other are Halle and Kim—my mom is Kim and I'm Halle, because those are the names of each of our best friends from Omaha! My mom was that person who always knew what I needed, when I needed it, and how to help. She started dancing when she was three, and she was eighteen when she started her studio (it was

# How do you (marsh)MELLOW out?

Name your favorite ways to relax!

. . . . . . . . . . . . . . . . . . . . . . . . . . . . . . . . . . . . . . . . . . . . . . . . . . . .

. . . . . . . . . . . . . . . . . . . . . . . . . . . . . . . . . . . . . . . . . . . . . . . . . . . .

. . . . . . . . . . . . . . . . . . . . . . . . . . . . . . . . . . . . . . . . . . . . . . . . . . . .

. . . . . . . . . . . . . . . . . . . . . . . . . . . . . . . . . . . . . . . . . . . . . . . . . . . .

. . . . . . . . . . . . . . . . . . . . . . . . . . . . . . . . . . . . . . . . . . . . . . . . . . . .

. . . . . . . . . . . . . . . . . . . . . . . . . . . . . . . . . . . . . . . . . . . . . . . . . . . .

. . . . . . . . . . . . . . . . . . . . . . . . . . . . . . . . . . . . . . . . . . . . . . . . . . . .

. . . . . . . . . . . . . . . . . . . . . . . . . . . . . . . . . . . . . . . . . . . . . . . . . . . .

either that or be a doctor!) so she totally gets it. She's an amazing mom. We have a ritual that goes like this: She says, "I love you!" And I say, "I love you more." Then she replies with, "Not possible!" And I say, "Oh, yes it is!"

We balance each other, and make each other laugh, even when things go wrong. So . . . here's a secret: I'm deathly afraid of tornado sirens, which we hear a lot in Nebraska. Or really any danger siren, if I'm honest. This one night not too long ago, the fire alarm went off in our apartment complex in LA. It was nearly 4 A.M.! I woke up, grabbed the dog, and *ran* out of our apartment without my mom—every man for himself! Then my mom woke up and called after me to come back in, and told me not to panic. We figured it was probably a small fire—someone's toaster oven maybe. My mom said, "Don't freak out, JoJo! Don't panic!" But then I went out on the deck and saw all the people gathered downstairs, and I lost it! I screamed, "Is there a fiiiiiire????" Just sheer panic! I was terrified!

No one answered me, and my mom said, "JoJo, I told you not to panic!" But she was laughing because I was so over-the-top about it. We wound up going downstairs and waiting in the cold with everyone else—and of course there was no fire. Better safe than sorry.

## Our family is always laughing.
## We love to tease each other.

My entire family snores, but my dad and I love to give my mom a hard time about it. One night, the two of us were awake, and I was playing on my phone when my mom fell asleep on the sofa and started to snore. Five minutes later, her own snoring woke her up and she sort of nudged my dad and said, "Tom! Stop snoring!" But he wasn't even asleep yet! Now we laugh about it all the time, and it's turned into an ongoing joke. Now if my mom's teasing my dad about something we say, "Oh, should he stop snoring?" We have all kinds of family jokes like that.

When my mom and I aren't doing work stuff, we like to have chill days by the pool or hang out and watch *Grey's Anatomy* or just not do anything the whole day— those are my favorite types of days. My mom loves to go to movies, but movies are my least favorite things to watch! For her birthday last year, I gave her a few free passes: one was to take me to her favorite (and my least favorite) restaurant—sushi! One was a whole day of doing whatever she wants, and the last one was a movie pass.

WE BALANCE EACH OTHER, AND MAKE EACH OTHER LAUGH, EVEN WHEN THINGS GO WRONG.

It's been just the two of us for a long time. That wasn't the original plan—but we've moved to both Pittsburgh and California, and we've done two TV shows, and we've become sort of a duo. Because my brother, Jayden, is still in school in Omaha, my dad lives out there with him—but they both come visit a lot, and we go back to Nebraska whenever we can! When my dad's in town or we're in Omaha, we play Dr. Mario sometimes on an old Nintendo. It started out as a competition between my mom and my dad, but then I started to play and I got addicted! Now they can't beat me, and it makes them so mad.

Since I like to stay home rather than go out, my mom and I do all kinds of fun activities together.

When we first started selling my bows, we created them together! We went to get ribbon colors we liked, we designed them, and we predicted that mint would be a fun, up-and-coming color (sure enough it was!). We picked the tie-dyed ribbon and the birthday bow. We even do puzzles at night while we eat dinner, and we like to play cards. When it's the whole family together, sometimes we go to theme parks or baseball games. And my dad will drop everything to be with me if I want to do something like go on a bike ride!

Although my mom and I are a perfect pair, my personality is so like my dad's! People who haven't met my dad yet assume I'm my mom's mini-me because I look just like her. But my dad and I are just the same! We're super active—we just like to get stuff done. Even when we just hang out, we're usually doing active stuff. We go to a water park in Nebraska called CoCo Key—I used to love going there with him! We have a great time together, but sometimes it gets us into trouble!

One time when I was really little, I tagged along with my dad to the gym. I went on the treadmill, and because I didn't really know how to work it, I started going super fast, and I fell.

The treadmill was still running, and my knees were skidding across it . . . it was a total disaster! I was terrified. When my dad realized what was happening, he came to my rescue. He scooped me up in his arms just like I scoop up my dog BowBow sometimes. I was totally fine—just a little scared. Then we made a pact not to tell my mom—we all laugh about it now!

Actually, I used to lie to my mom a lot about stuff like that. I was always afraid she'd get worried or get mad at me for being too rough. Once when I was eight, I went to a trampoline park and broke my pinkie. I told my mom I shut it in a car door, but actually I'd played dodgeball with a giant sumo wrestler at the trampoline park. When the sumo wrestler threw the ball, he smashed my pinkie! I taped it to a Popsicle stick until it healed, and for the longest time my mom had no idea how I really broke it.

My dad and I love to hang out—we're really funny together. We both love to play games and work out, and he's always egging me on by saying, "You're so much like me." He's more like a friend than a parent! If I want something, I usually just go to my dad. If my mom said no, my dad will probably say yes. If I want to take a day off dancing to play with my friends, he'll say to my mom, "Just let her stay home and play!" And when people have teased me for my speech or my accent, my dad will say, "I love your little voice! Let's not change it!" He's always in my corner. Both my parents like to tell me and my brother that nobody's perfect. They always try to be natural parents, and they think messing up is part of what makes you who you are.

So my dad and me, we're two peas in a pod.
It's a good thing we have my brother and my
mom to keep us grounded!

But I've never consider myself a "daddy's little girl," because that's just not my personality and that's not our relationship. Once, a songwriter I was working with pitched that as an idea for a song, and we tried it out, but it never really worked because it wasn't *real*. I've never been that pampered-princess type!

Since my dad and brother technically live in Nebraska, I usually like to let my mom and dad have a little date night when he's in Los Angeles, since they don't get to see each other often. (True story:

My parents met through one of my mom's dance students when she was twenty-one!) My dad and I have our own special nights together too—we love going out to lunch or dinner, and one of our favorites is Panera. Usually we like to make a day of it because we don't see each other much—and my mom is the same with Jayden. When they're together, they make it extra special.

Jayden is a sophomore in high school, and we've been close our entire lives. We are exactly 2 years and 364 days apart—his birthday is May 20 and mine is May 19. There's a name for that, right? Some sort of twin? No? Well . . . there should be, because we're crazy close. When we were little, we used to wish there was just one day in between our birthdays so we could celebrate together on the middle day, in addition to having our own separate birthdays to

enjoy. It's so hard being away from him because he's my best friend, but we make it work. He comes to LA as much as he can—usually at least once a month.

We call him Jay or Jaybird and he and my parents call me Yoder or YoYo or Pojie Pot Pie. My mom says Jay loved me and protected me from day one—he was determined not to let anyone hurt me. If we go somewhere together, he keeps an eye on me—he'll protect me or die trying!

We like to swim in our pool and go to escape rooms, which are really popular in LA. The way they work is, you're locked in a room for an hour and have to uncover all the clues in order to unlock the door before time runs out! They're super hard, but so far we've always made it out on time.

All of Jayden's baseball friends became my friends too! Back in Omaha, his team would come over for parties and all the dancers would come over for parties, and we'd just mix everyone together. Everyone was always at our house, and we loved it. Once I even went to school with Jayden for a day—*that's* how much I love him. We were back in Omaha visiting, so I sat in on his classes and ate lunch with him. Then I remembered exactly how much I like to be homeschooled.

My brother has the sweetest, politest, easiest disposition. He's one of the most polite people you'll ever meet and the best big brother you could possibly think of! He's kind to everyone, and he'd do anything for his friends or family. He's also a good student—he's like the perfect kid! He used to hang around my grandma a lot when we were younger, so we think some of her personality rubbed off on him. He was always over at their house because he went to school near where they lived, so he'd go over there and help her make banana muffins and hamburger dip and beef stew, and they became very close. Now Jayden loves to cook! He makes stuff like prime rib—all the fancy food—whereas I'm more of a Kraft mac 'n' cheese kind of girl. Jayden is the king of the Grandma Rule. Don't know what that is? The Grandma Rule basically says, if you wouldn't say or do it around your grandma, don't do it at all.

Jayden and I play a lot of video games together. We love playing the Wii and baseball. We also *love* practical jokes. One year we put a fake snake in our pool—it was the type that expands in water;

THE GRANDMA RULE BASICALLY SAYS, IF YOU WOULDN'T SAY OR DO IT AROUND YOUR GRANDMA, DON'T DO IT AT ALL.

so when my dad opened up the pool cover, there was a big snake in there! He was like, "There's a snake in here—we've never had a snake before!" It was pretty funny until he figured it out.

Jayden is amazing at baseball—he wants to be either a baseball player or a chef when he's older. At one point we were going through a phase when Jayden had baseball all the time and did a lot of working out, but let his grades slip. He got three C's on his progress report—and my parents said he could only stay in Nebraska if he brought his grades back up. They joked that the three C's stood for, "It'll be *challenging* to *convince* us to *continue* staying here." My brother picked his grades back up after that—he loves his school and his friends!

I love Nebraska too. My favorite thing when I'm back in Omaha—besides hanging out with all my friends—is to watch my brother play baseball. In fact, we plan our trips back to Omaha around it! If we're deciding between two weekends, we'll always go for the one when he has baseball. Jayden's so talented, and I love going to his games and taking a million pictures or even just messing with the team at the dugout. Pretty sure I'm his biggest fan.

We have fun together no matter what we're doing. In our Omaha house, there's a man cave and a dance room. The man cave is where all my brother's stuff and dad's stuff are—like the pool table and arcade games and Ping-Pong table. In the dance room, there are mirrors on one wall, a mounted ballet bar, a wall shelf filled with scrapbooks, and a wall displaying trophies and costumes. It's sort of the perfect kid utopia down there. We can do anything and be totally happy.

At Christmas we used to do a themed tree. One year, my brother decided to mix it up. Jayden considers himself a sneaker-head—he's obsessed with sneakers and knows all about them!—so we created a tree that had shoes on it: We tied the shoes together and looped them over the tree. He started it as a joke and then I said, "Let's actually do it!" So we went for it, and my mom let us keep it up! Nothing is ever "typical" at our house!

Obviously because we're siblings, sometimes Jayden and I get mad at each other . . . but we really don't fight. We just know it's wrong, so we don't do it—easy as that. But he *does* do annoying things just to get under my skin. Like, he has this weird deep-breathing thing he does that really bugs me. This long wheeze. He'll do it just to make me mad; but even though I'm mad, it's sort of funny, since he's just messing with me.

**65**

And for my part, he can't stand it when I boss him around. (Which is never, because what kind of sister would do that?) Really, he's the most unconditionally loving brother ever. Like I said . . . lucky!

## My brother always says, "What's cuter than a teacup Yorkie? A fat teacup Yorkie!"

We have three dogs total and I love them all, but the one that's all mine is BowBow—and she *loves sugar*. She eats cupcakes! We share drinks! She'll even drink Sunny D out of the squirt bottle. And she loves marshmallows. She likes healthy food too—she'll chomp on a carrot like a rabbit. But when she goes to her babysitter's, we joke around that she comes back a few pounds lighter—no people food over there!

BowBow is my little girl. She's great at learning tricks. Her favorite is to roll over; she also loves giving high-fives and kisses. She's also into dressing up! She has lots of loves in the world—including a little pink monster—a little gorilla that's like her baby. But her favorite thing in the whole wide world is me.

We get in barking wars. She never barks normally, but if I go, "Ruff!" she'll do it back. We snuggle up and sleep together every single night, and she likes to lie right between my legs or with her back end right in my face. BowBow and our other dogs, CoCo and LuLu, round out our perfect little family. I couldn't love them more!

# JOJO'S GUIDE
## TO BEING A GREAT
## FAMILY MEMBER

# Love every minute.

Since half my family lives in Nebraska and half lives in California, it's very difficult for us to give a hug every day or say goodnight in person every night. But what's really cool is that we have FaceTime, so we can still see each other. I love calling my brother every day—asking him how school is, how his grades are, how baseball is going. We love talking to each other. It's one of those things . . . your family is your family. You have a right to get mad at your family, but not to disrespect. Agree to disagree! No matter what happens, your family is always there for you. Your family will catch you when you fall, will bring you up when you're down, will tell you the truth. Your family is always honest. Your family will always be there for you. Through fire, ice, big bows, and small bows.

## Every family is different.

My family, in my opinion, is perfect. But even though we're perfect, there are still things that are tough. My grandma died last year. It was horrible for my family. My other

grandma is having heart issues this year. It's so hard. Some families don't have a mom or dad, or a brother or sister. Some families are adopted. But most families have one person (or animal!) in them to be close to. Know who your people are. Family isn't necessarily about blood. It's about the people who are *your* people. The ones you can count on. The people who are closest to you—your role models, your go-tos.

It goes without saying that "family" can be defined a million different ways. I have friends who are adopted; friends who are closer to their cousins than their siblings;

and friends who have become an extension of my own family. My *Dance Moms* family will always be in my heart, and although my Nickelodeon family is new to me, I can already tell they're going to be a part of my life forever! The most important thing is to surround yourself with people you love, trust, and can rely on. Be ready—they'll come into your life in unexpected ways!

# Be supportive.

Your family is always there for you—so why wouldn't you always be there for them? If your brother has a baseball game, go cheer him on! Or maybe your baby sister has a dance recital. Be there for her—help her practice her dance, run the music, cheer your family on. That's the number one thing! Where would I be if my family hadn't shown up at my dance competitions when I was little, or at the Kids' Choice Awards when I won? Who would I be if I hadn't spent a million hours cheering Jayden on at baseball? Or hung out with my dad at the gym? Or told all my secrets to my mom and kept all of hers? I would not be the same JoJo! Part of being in a family is being there for each other—so support the people you love.

# 4

# Dreamsicle

#KeepingItCool

# AT SOME POINT WE ALL HAVE TO GROW UP.

**AND IT DIDN'T TAKE ME LONG AFTER** my first solo to understand competitions were about more than applause and beautiful costumes. That lesson happened when I got into the AMTC competition.

When I was five, my mom heard an ad on the radio about a talent competition for actors, models, and dancers called AMTC. It was one of those events that advertised—we were driving around and my mom heard, "Does your kid have what it takes to be a star?" And so she took Jayden and me straight to the mall to audition!

It turned out the recruiters loved both of us—but I was the one who wound up going to Florida for a big competition that involved singing and dancing and headshots and monologues and even a mock-TV commercial. There were agents and casting people there, and the idea was that they'd call back if they were interested in representing us.

AMTC is a big deal. Lots of kids who compete end up as famous actors, dancers, and models. Even now, I'll meet some cool young actor from Nickelodeon, and somehow it will come up. "Wait," they'll say, "you went to AMTC too?"

When I was accepted, I was excited, mainly because our hotel would have a pool, and I'd get to wear my favorite polka-dotted

bathing suit. Meeting new people, performing for an audience, *and* splashing around? Who was I to turn that down?

After months of classes preparing us for Orlando, we arrived. There must have been a thousand people in line to check in that first day! That's when I realized this wasn't all about my cute bathing suit. Judging by the expressions around me, AMTC was *serious business*. There were a ton of kids, and most of them were older than me. Everyone had way bigger dreams than room service cheeseburgers and lounging by the pool.

AMTC took three days and was packed with competitions. Not only did I get to dance, I was able to do all the fun stuff too!

The first day was amazing, as I ran from place to place, performing for new audiences every time. Everyone was having fun, and I got a ton of callbacks! In the end, the judges picked their favorite contestants to sing and dance in the showcase . . . and they picked

# What's YOUR "Baby Diva" moment?

Write down a time when you had
fun being in the spotlight!

me! My mom called my dad and told him to hop on the next flight over so he could watch.

There I was, center stage and three feet shorter than anyone else. I made an entrance with my side ponytail topped off with a big red bow. I was only five, but could already rock that look. I *owned* that dance.

And afterward, everyone went totally crazy!

My solo wasn't long—thirty seconds, max, and then I was racing offstage. But the audience kept cheering long after I disappeared!

I was a star that day. And for the first time, I really knew what that meant—and the pressures that came with it. Everyone congratulated me, and I felt really proud. But then something unexpected happened. When they presented the awards for my age group, I won in every single category except . . .

*Dance.*

## Now we all laugh about the fact that the only category I didn't win was the category I came for!

It's funny to think back on it now, but the thing is, I always tried my best. I never messed around, not even back then when I was just starting out! Nothing major came directly from AMTC—but it was so valuable anyway. We met all kinds of people, and even got a callback from a manager, Marcia Weisman. We went to LA and met with some agents, and signed with LA Models the summer before I

I WAS A STAR THAT DAY. AND FOR THE FIRST TIME, I REALLY KNEW WHAT THAT MEANT—AND THE PRESSURES THAT CAME WITH IT.

started kindergarten. From there we did all kinds of auditions. For a little while we lived in Palm Springs and would go to huge auditions for companies like Nestlé with nearly a thousand girls lined up.

When you're a kid, you have this dream that you'll show up at a competition and get picked up by some major company and become a star. But it doesn't work like that—it takes a lot more time, and a lot of work. It's important to remember that, so you don't put too much pressure on yourself to achieve your dreams right away or every time. Even though I didn't book anything then, we learned so much through the people we met—it was sort of a preview of what would happen for me later. And because of it, we were better prepared when the time came.

AMTC taught me there was more to dance than just having fun. For the big kids, dancing wasn't about one routine . . . it was about their futures. Maybe it was mine too. But if so, there'd be a lot of "new" moments ahead . . . and a lot of times where I'd have to teach myself how to stay calm under pressure.

I didn't win the dance award at AMTC, but I got something even better: my destiny. That's the moment I realized dance was bigger than a competition or even showcase.

I had no idea where dance would take me,
but I couldn't wait to find out.

# JOJO'S GUIDE TO KEEPING IT COOL

20

JoJo Siwa

# Know it'll be okay.

Everyone will both win and lose at some point in their lives. You never know when your loss is going to come, but eventually it'll be there. What I'd tell you guys is that it'll always be okay—because if even this time it doesn't work out how you think it should, you'll be fine—you'll go home to your friends and family! Always be confident in yourself, and know that no matter the result, you're an amazing person who is surrounded by love. No matter what the outcome, you'll be okay. I've lost plenty of competitions in my day—and I got through it! Not only that: I didn't let it stop me. No one was telling me I *had* to win or *had* to be the best—quite the opposite! That's why internal pressure to succeed every single time wasn't necessary. Once I learned to shake it loose—and once I stopped putting tons of pressure on the outcome—everything got a whole lot easier.

# Get back up.

Trust me, I know it can be hard to get back up when you're down. You've gotta know who to surround yourself with—you've got your friends and family to help you. You might think to yourself, "Why should I get back up? Why should I finish what I started?" It's important not to let setbacks ruin your confidence, because they're temporary—and you're stronger than that.

## Realize your mistakes.

Usually when something doesn't work out the way I planned, there was a mistake or two in there. (Or let's be real, a few hundred.) If something went wrong, work

harder next time. Abby Lee Miller sometimes says, "Today is not your day." Even if there was no mistake and you did the very best you could, keep practicing! It might just not have been your day!

## Go easy on yourself.

Even if it's not your day in one particular way, find a way to make it great! Say you don't win at a tennis match—shake it off and hang out with your friends! Have fun! At the end of every day, I ask myself, "If today was my last day, would I be happy with how I spent it?" And if my answer is no, I do something to fix that! Even if it's the worst day possible, I'll go home and watch my favorite TV show! I'll chill with my friends! I'll make it a really fun day and just find a positive.

## Go get ice cream.

This chapter guide is called "JoJo's Guide to Keeping It Cool" for a reason! It's about staying cool under pressure . . . So what better way to stay cool than getting ice cream?! Or a snow cone. Or a Popsicle. Or anything chilly. Anything your heart desires! It's all about staying cool.

# 5

# Life Savers

#WhenLifeThrowsACurveball

# LET'S BE HONEST!

**AFTER MY BIG "BABY DIVA" SOLO** and the AMTC, there was no turning back. From there on out, I was obsessed with dancing! As for my mom, she was right there supporting me. She's always believed in my dreams, from the time I was little to this very day. She saw that dancing made me confident and happy, and that's what matters most.

If you go to a lot of dance competitions or watch *Dance Moms*, you know how tough some moms can be. Sometimes I see kids backstage who obviously don't want to be there. They hate missing stuff for rehearsals and would rather spend the weekend hanging with their BFFs. I always feel bad for them . . . you shouldn't put so much time into something unless you love it! Lucky for me, my mom never pushed me to be anything other than what I choose to be.

Sometimes it's easy to forget the people around us, supporting us every day. And most moms are like mine—loving their kid and wanting them to be happy! This book is about appreciating your true self and the people who let you be that way! Now I know to appreciate my mom for everything she's done. Even if tomorrow I decided I wanted to be a rock star, doctor, or president, she'd be right there encouraging me.

So, growing up I always wanted to dance. Right?

Mostly right. Because I wanted to do a lot of other stuff too!

My brother, Jayden, always played baseball—so when I was six, I decided I wanted to play baseball too! I loved softball! I was a catcher and right fielder, so I'd have to throw the ball as hard as I could—and let me tell you, I can throw that ball so far.

When I first started softball, my dad put his foot down. Even though he coached Jayden's team, he didn't want to coach girls! He thought softball wouldn't be as exciting as baseball. But in the end, he wound up helping out with the team—all the coaches were friends, and he couldn't help himself! Plus, when he saw how good I was, he wanted to get involved. Best of all? He realized softball was way more fun than he expected!

One day at a tournament, we were tied and my coach put me in to pitch. He whispered to my parents, "She's our secret weapon!"

It felt so good to hear that, especially since I was new. I had the best time playing softball—I even played on the all-star team and was asked to play on the select team. I had my mom paint my helmet lime green and black with sparkles!

# Do you play a SPORT?

What inspires you to do your best when you're
on the court/field/dance floor/gym floor?
Who are your athlete inspirations?

. . . . . . . . . . . . . . . . . . . . . . . . . . . . . . . . . . .

. . . . . . . . . . . . . . . . . . . . . . . . . . . . . . . . . . .

. . . . . . . . . . . . . . . . . . . . . . . . . . . . . . . . . . .

. . . . . . . . . . . . . . . . . . . . . . . . . .

. . . . . . . . . . . . . . . . . . . . . . . . .

. . . . . . . . . . . . . . . . . . . . . . . .

. . . . . . . . . . . . . . . . . . . . . . . .

. . . . . . . . . . . . . . . . . . . . . . .

. . . . . . . . . . . . . . . . . . . . . .

# What's your POWER outfit or accessory?

## Draw a picture below!

And I made awesome friends.

I did join the select team, but I left when I was seven because it was a fast-pitch league, and I got scared. I knew it was okay to quit, because the team wasn't going to be happy with me in the end if I didn't want to be there. And my parents supported it, because they'd never make me or Jayden do anything we didn't want to do—no matter how talented!

Softball wasn't the only thing I tried out. I joined a competitive cheer team around that same time! It involved lots of gymnastics and tumbling—but one night, at parent night, my dad got really upset watching the performance. He came home to my mom and said, "If they drop her on her head one more time, she's done. There's too much to lose—we only have one daughter!" My mom agreed, and we decided I would stop then before I could get hurt. But I don't regret trying it for a second.

Even now, I'm all about trying out new sports. I've learned to throw a football in a spiral, and I can sink a basketball from almost anywhere. When I go to parties now and there's a basketball court, I'll get right out there with the boys, even if they're way older than I am! I have so much fun challenging myself.

I think one of the most important things a person can do is take risks—and not be afraid to try new things.

# JOJO'S GUIDE
## TO
## TRYING NEW THINGS

# Never be afraid.

Trust me, I'm one of the most loyal people ever. I'm loyal to my friends. But I'm also really loyal to the things I commit to. So for example, my four ponytail holders: I wear the same exact four ponytail holders every day of my life: pink, yellow, orange, and lime green. But even though I'm so loyal—trust me when I say this—I have fun trying new things! Sure, sometimes it won't go smoothly. But other times it's going to be amazing! So you can't ever be afraid to try football if you're a tiny little dancer, or try sushi if you've never touched raw fish! Don't be afraid to experience all the different things out there, and learn what you like! #NeverBeAfraid

# Be honest.

Life is short! Life as we know it, anyway . . . #YOLO! So you have to know what you like. If you're going through a phase in your life where you love this one TV show and don't want to watch anything else . . . just enjoy the TV show! Don't watch something else to be cool or fit in. Enjoy what you love while it lasts! Always be honest with yourself. Don't be afraid to tell your mom or dad or teacher or guardian if you don't like something. Everyone wants you to be happy! If you're not happy doing whatever you're doing, tell someone—they may be able to help you find your right fit. It can be so scary to admit to *yourself* what you want, let alone your parents! But life is short— don't spend time on "what-ifs."

## Know it's not gonna be perfect.

Nothing's perfect. Nobody's perfect. There's always going to be some kind of bump in the road. But know that when you're going through that phase where things aren't perfectly smooth . . . there will be another time in your future where you'll be happy and excited.

Remember that when a door closes, another door opens. And starting over is all about the learning curve!

# 6
# Nerds
# & Smarties

#BookWormz

# HERE'S A NOT-SO-SECRET.

**ONE OF MY FAVORITE THINGS** in the world is school.

I'm really good at math, and sometimes I spend hours researching how to use the latest video- and photo-editing software, just because I want to. Whoever gave nerds a bad rap obviously never felt the joy of spending three hours producing and editing their own YouTube video . . . just saying!

Have you ever noticed how people are afraid to talk about this stuff? I'm not saying I'm a super genius. (Let's be honest, we all have "duh" moments.) I'm not saying I'm a rocket scientist (though that would be awesome) or that I'm any better than all my brilliant and talented friends. What makes me different is that I'm proud of my intelligence and not afraid to say it! Hence why I'm writing a book! (Why are people so afraid to admit it's fun to read?)

I want to tell you about being homeschooled, because sometimes I talk with people who think being homeschooled is weird. (Let's be honest, they're probably jealous that I get to go to school in my pajamas!)

hours on set. On weekends, I don't have to, because no one does school on weekends.

We have a private teacher who comes to the house. The beauty about homeschool is that I don't have to do the class projects—busywork that takes up a lot of time.

It's always been my dream to be something *big*. I've made it my goal to become a pop star. Lots of people want to be famous, but not everyone understands that in order to be really good at anything, you have to be willing to work hard and be a little different and embrace your inner nerd. You have to give it your best effort in order to achieve your dreams! With my mom, on the dance team, I'd put in twenty-five hours per week. With my other goals it's no different!

Maybe that sounds tough—but if you want it bad enough, it doesn't feel like hard work. Find that thing you love and go after it, Siwanatorz! Hard work is the absolute opposite of boring and nerdy if you have a passion! When my mom homeschooled me, she taught me to follow my dreams. She encouraged me to pick the subjects that interested me and pour everything into them. Sometimes that meant learning the tech skills I use today to edit my YouTube videos. Other times it was about making room in my schedule for dance each and every day.

Now I have a million goals. One thing I learned from being on *Dance Moms* and *Abby's Ultimate Dance Competition* is not just how to dream . . . but how to make my dreams into reality. Once you achieve one tough goal, the door opens wide—you know anything's possible! But you have to know how to get there.

That's why I always have a plan.

Some people prefer to be spontaneous, and that's amazing too—random fun always has its place. (You're talking to the girl who dumps juice on her head, come on.)

But for me it's weird. I can be fun/random/spontaneous/silly . . . and also have a plan for what I'm doing for the next five years.

# What are your GOALS?

One of my goals is to buy a house one day. Another is to make new friends. List three of your goals below!

I'm not kidding, I have a plan through when I'm eighteen . . . even longer. I plan tomorrow, the next day, and years from now. That's because what I do today, tomorrow, and the next day will *always* impact where I'm at later on.

My Big Plan (the years from now part) involves my own goals— what I want out of my career—but also the people I love most. Because nothing would be possible without my family. They rock. Do you have any guesses for what one of my biggest goals could be? Hint . . . it involves all of us—my mom, my dad, me, and my brother, Jayden—and all our dogs (plus maybe a couple more, cause there's no such thing as too many furry friends) right here in LA with a giant backyard and a whole room just for the dogs.

Yes, I'm fourteen and I want to buy a house. Not just any house— my dream house. So, maybe that's a bigger goal than most kids my age have. But I know that with hard work, I can do it! What are your goals? Goals don't have to be as big as buying a house. They can be simple stuff that doesn't involve money at all—like making a new friend, or acing your math test or beating your personal best on the swim team or even just doing something nice for someone you love.

That's why goals are kind of the best. They can be anything, no matter how big or small, and you feel great when you make them come true!

# JOJO'S GUIDE TO STAYING SMART

# Be real.

I'm a very techy person. I love all things to do with computers. So what I did is, I asked my mom (who is my principal, since I am homeschooled!) to add a computer class into my curriculum. It took a whole year of learning how to edit—I produced my own song (the *JoJo's Juice* song). I wrote it in one night! I did it just like that. I love to do my own YouTube editing and create my own thumbnails, because it's fun for me! A lot of my friends will call me and say, "Hey, how do I fix this issue for my computer?" They'll want to know how to force quit or delete something . . . and I know all the answers because I love computers!

In today's generation there's a lot we can do with technology. We have iPhones and laptops and Apple TVs—a lot of fancy, smart technology right now. I wanted to learn more about it because it's something that interested me. Find whatever interests *you* and go after it—learn as much as you can about it!

# LEARNING on your own IS FUN!

Here are some ideas for projects you can do outside of school:

- Learn origami
- Learn how to say "hello" in three new languages
- Design a dream house and build it out of cardboard boxes, or draw a picture of it
- Plant an herb garden with an adult
- Create a terrarium
- Make a "museum" of your favorite things or memories (tickets you've saved, autographs you've gotten), set them up in a display, and take a friend on a tour

# Take corrections!

If someone's giving you a correction, it's a good thing. It means they're paying attention, and want you to get better. I always say, *take a correction and apply it*. If you're not sure about the correction, ask for help! There's nothing wrong with asking for help. Most of all, always say thank you! You shouldn't ever be hurt by a correction, because almost all the time it's for your own good.

# Plan ahead.

When I plan ahead, I don't just plan what I'm doing tomorrow—I also plan what I'm doing five years from now. It's something different about me, and I like being different! I plan five years from now because I like to know my future. In five years I'll be about nineteen. I'm probably going to be living my life and having fun. I'll be able to drive by then! When I'm nineteen, I'll still be living with my mom—but I'm going to be doing music and acting. I can picture it really vividly. What I see in my mind is the exact song I'll be singing, and my exact costumes on my tour. Seeing such a vivid picture in my head helps me do what I need to do *now* to get to that point later!

# Study.

If you want to learn new skills, you have to study and practice. I didn't just wake up one day and magically know how to edit a YouTube video. Trust me, I wasn't that great at editing when I first started! But now, after a year of studying, I've learned! I'm never going to stop learning. Beyond just the skills you want to develop, it's important to be curious about the world and the people in it. Sometimes that just means reading something interesting or asking someone about their culture—education doesn't have to happen just in a classroom!

## Don't be scared of being smart.

It's never a bad thing to be smart! Sure, if you're the smart girl in school, you're gonna get a little hate. But it all goes back to my song "Boomerang"—don't listen to what the haters say! I love books. If someone asked me what my favorite activities are, I'd say the three S's: "Singing, swimming, school."

# And that, Siwanatorz, is what it takes to be a nerd . . . ahem, cool. (If you didn't know you could be cool and a nerd at the same time, now you do!)

When's the last time you felt proud of being smart or reaching a goal? Shout it out on Twitter or Instagram with #LifeGoals, and I'll do the same. Ready . . . go!

# 7

# Kit-Kat

## #GimmeABreak(Through)

# A FEW YEARS AFTER I QUIT SOFTBALL I GOT MY FIRST BIG BREAK!

**I WAS CHOSEN TO APPEAR** on *Abby's Ultimate Dance Competition* (AUDC). My mom and I were huge fans of the show, and of Abby Lee Miller's work. So when my mom was watching *Dance Moms* in Omaha one night and saw an ad at the bottom of the screen for AUDC Season 2, she jumped on it. She didn't even ask me—she just filled out the paperwork and sent in a video of me dancing!

Later that afternoon she went to lunch with my aunt; when she got home from lunch that very same day, she had a voice mail from a casting director saying, "I want to talk to you about getting JoJo on the show!" When my mom broke the news, we were doing laps around the house and screaming—we were so excited! So my mom called him back and he asked us to do a Skype interview. Since we were going on vacation the next day, we had to wait a whole week for that interview. Then we scrambled all around preparing for it— there was a whole setup they asked for! We had to put trophies in the background, and I had to wear a full costume and makeup. We did everything we had to do. We were so ready.

Then, just when everything was set up and we were about to dial in, the casting director called. He was sick and couldn't make it! By then, it felt like we'd been waiting so long that we were kind of over it. The next day when we did the rescheduled Skype interview, I wasn't nervous at all—and it turned out to be an *amazing* audition.

We hit it off like we were old friends. The casting director, RJ, loved us!

But then time passed—a lot of time—and we still hadn't heard from him.

After about a month and a half, when we were sure I hadn't made it, RJ finally called back! He said, "You're going to New York! There's a final callback in New York City!"

So they flew us to New York and put us up in a nice hotel right across the street from Madison Square Garden. It was my first time in New York! It was so exciting, and such a big deal for us. We had to bring a costume, and there was even a live interview. All the moms even had to take tests to make sure they'd be okay appearing on TV!

The morning after that, we were both really tired but had to get with it for my interview. So my mom texted RJ and said, "JoJo and I need sodas"—and he had an assistant send them over! Then he

# TYPICALLY I'LL DO PRETTY MUCH WHATEVER MY MOM ASKS ME TO DO!

said, "I want you guys to walk into that interview with your matching sodas."

We started getting ready—my mom was helping me do my hair and makeup—and all of a sudden I felt dizzy and sick. I turned white and grabbed the sink hard. It was just nerves—but for a split second I felt like I was going to pass out, and I was due to interview in just a couple of minutes!

Luckily it passed, and by the time I got downstairs I was totally fine. The interview was in a big ballroom in the hotel. The producers said, "When you open the door, you'll be on camera." I had never been on TV in my life, and all of a sudden I was about to open the door to a ballroom with a bunch of paparazzi waiting!

My mom jumped right in the second we opened the door—she started with, "Okay JoJo, warm up, do your stretch!" And I was like, "I'm good, I already did it!" My mom was so not used to me saying no. Typically I'll do pretty much whatever my mom asks me to do! But the producers *loved* it—and like RJ predicted, they also loved our matching sodas.

Then I did my dance and it was great. The producers had wanted me to do jazz or lyrical, but that year all I'd done was contemporary and musical theater. My mom was worried she'd have to teach me a whole new dance before the interview—but I pulled an old one out of my back pocket, my solo from the year before. Luckily, I remembered it really well.

They had a million questions for us, and I was my usual funny self! They kept asking a bunch of leading questions, like, "JoJo, what's it like to dance at your mom's studio? Do you fight with the other girls?" I was totally confident in all my answers, and they *loved* it! Later, we realized I was the only tiny girl in the whole place. It was almost as if they already knew they were going to cast me in that role.

After it was all over, I was wiped out. But my mom wasn't going to let me miss out on my first time in New York City! She took me everywhere—on the subway, to Madison Square Garden, all the way downtown . . . I even got a foam Statue of Liberty hat! She dragged me all around that day, but we had so much fun!

After we went back to Nebraska, a couple of weeks went by. Again, we weren't sure if we'd made it. We weren't even sure at that point if the show was going to happen at all! Then one day, we were in the parking lot of the homeschool store when a weird number popped up on my mom's phone. She picked it up, and it was the show!

"I just wanted to tell you: You're going to be on the show," they said.

I started crying, I was so happy—and I practically *never* cry! It was the best phone call ever. After that, what did we do?

We went shopping, of course! We had tons to prepare for. We had forty custom dance outfits made. Then one day my mom thought, "You know what? I'll have forty custom hair bows made to match those outfits!"

Finally the day arrived: We flew out to LA. As soon as we got to our hotel, the producers whisked us up to our hotel room and told us we couldn't leave! They even brought us our meals! So we unpacked and got settled in—we had no idea what was coming next.

The next day, they brought us in to shoot the opener for the show. They took headshots, then escorted us straight back up to our rooms, so we couldn't talk to anyone or see who else was going to be on the show.

The day after that, they said, "You're coming to set today. Check out of your room and bring all your luggage with you." They were moving us to the apartments they had on set! There it was, day three—and we were moving into the bungalows. We filmed all day that day. We met all the other contestants too. They put us on stage and said, "Okay kids, warm up!" And then we had to warm up for two and a half hours!

I'm competitive and of course I wanted to win . . . but I also wanted to make friends! And I knew my mom did too. So when I met a really nice girl and hit it off, the two of us went up to our moms and said, "We're going to be friends, so you have to be friends too!" That's how my mom and I met Kalani and Kira, who would go on to be on *Dance Moms* with us, and to become some of our closest friends.

That same night, the producers took us to our rooms. Each room had a star on the door with a contestant's name.

We walked up to the first house. The rooms were so tiny, almost like cruise ship's cabins! And the bathrooms were outdoors, almost like outhouses! Luckily our names were not on those doors.

The next house was the same situation. By then we were getting nervous—we were really going to have to rough it with those outhouses. But our names weren't on those doors either. Then we got to the third house. The third house was huge. There were four different apartments, a laundry room, a kitchen, and a nice

MEETING
ROOM 1

Jojo Siwa

In Use

bathroom. That's where we were staying! And best of all, Kira and Kalani had the adjoining apartment! We got the best apartments, hands down—we were so relieved.

With Kira and Kalani next door, we had tons of fun. We left the door connecting the apartments open—and every single morning Kalani would come into our rooms and talk to my mom while I slept. (I'm so not a morning person!) She'd sit on my feet and steal my blanket! She'd come snuggle in my bed with me until I woke up . . . and then at night everyone would come to our room to hang out, including security and cast and crew and cameramen. We'd hang out all night! We were kind of a loud group, always having fun. One night we were making videos to the Harlem Shake.

Our friends the Atwoods—Tyler and Travis, who are identical twins, and their mom, Cheryl—lived right underneath us. They tended to be on the quieter side, and probably got a little sick of hearing us laughing and dancing all the time! That night I shouted, "Kalani, I have a good idea, let's do this!" And Cheryl opened her door and shouted up, "JoJo, I have a good idea! Let's be quiet!!" It was hilarious. They were listening to books on tape while they fell asleep, and we were jamming out. The whole thing was so funny and so much fun—like being at summer camp with all your favorite people. And every day was something new.

My first solo ever on *AUDC* was "Rapunzel" for the theme "fairy tales come to life." It was a really good dance, but I had to wear a long wig in order to be the character, Rapunzel, from the fairy tale. It was tied right into my real hair and was heavy— and I had to go a solid week without washing my hair. You'd never know it from watching the video of the dance, but it's true!

Every three days at *AUDC*, there was an elimination. You just didn't know how long you'd be there— and we wound up living out of our suitcases rather than unpacking like we did at the hotel. We would go on Target runs and get enough food for just three days at a time, because you never knew how long you'd be around. It was so fun working with the cast, but then someone would get eliminated. Every three days we cried. When the person got eliminated, they took her away and took you away, so you couldn't even say goodbye.

Since we lived on set, we learned a lot about being on set. There was terminology we learned. *Hard ice* meant "Silence! No talking!" *Ice* meant we could talk quietly, but not about the show. *Pumpkin* was another word for "it's a wrap"—we were done for the day. *OTF* meant "on the fly." And my favorite—*chipmunking*—was a word for taking snacks from crafty. (*Crafty* was another word for the food we'd get on set!) After we were done shooting each day, the boys and the crew and I would play basketball at the hoops on set.

There was even a food truck! In the morning, Kalani and I would walk down to pick up whatever our moms wanted. Our call time would be around 9 A.M.—and Kira and my mom would just say, "We're not coming down, tell us whenever you need us!"

Travis Atwood and I were really good friends too. Sometimes we'd sneak out and go exploring. One night, we found other little dressing rooms on the set—they weren't for the cast; they were for the judges. We snuck around and saw the entire set before everyone else: the vanity room and living room and the kitchen that were all going to be on camera! I'd read the call sheets and see how long we were working the next day. We had the best time.

AFTER WE WERE DONE SHOOTING EACH DAY, THE BOYS AND THE CREW AND I WOULD PLAY BASKETBALL AT THE HOOPS ON SET.

Meeting Abby for the first time was incredible. We met her on that first day, when we were doing our two-hour improv. All of a sudden she appeared behind everyone—she was watching us, but we didn't know it. Then I figured it out and turned to face her to do my routine—no one else figured it out. My mom heard her say, "That little JoJo is the only one with common sense enough to turn around and face me."

My first experience being on TV was unbelievable. I made it to the top five, and I was so sad when I got eliminated—it was the day before my birthday!

Best tenth birthday present ever, right? But it's okay, everything happens for a reason. If I hadn't gotten fifth on *AUDC*, odds are I wouldn't be where I am today. I got far for a kid from Nebraska who'd trained in her mom's dance studio.

It was amazing to learn all the new dances. The dances were *hard*, by the way! We had only two days to learn each one—and only two hours with the choreographer each day! We could always practice on our own, so that's what everyone did at night in the empty rehearsal room.

One week, we were up there dancing on our own, preparing for the show on nightmares. We were listening to Trinity's song. The lyrics went, "There's an evil in the room . . ." And it was dark and creepy, and suddenly, we heard a *thud thud thud*. There was

someone running toward us from the top of the room, stomping down the stairs straight for us! It was terrifying. It turned out it was just a crew member—she'd been watching us for weeks before she decided to freak us out!

When I got eliminated, there was only one week left in the show; so we stayed for a week to do the final, wrap-up show. After the wrap-up, all of us went home . . . and about a month later the show started airing. No matter what, we couldn't tell people how I did— we were sworn to secrecy! So every week we'd have a viewing party at the bowling alley. We'd invite all our friends and watch it together and have fun!

# JOJO'S GUIDE TO BEING CONFIDENT

# Know who you are.

When I say, "Know yourself, know your name," I don't mean, "Know your name is JoJo Siwa." I mean, *know what it means to be you.* I know that being JoJo Siwa means I like to dance and act and wear my hair in a side ponytail. I know what I love and what I hate. You just always have to be yourself and know who you are—know what your feelings are: whether you like something or whether you want to do that thing you tried. Know the things that make you YOU.

The better you know yourself, the easier it'll be to be confident in your own skin.

# Put yourself out there.

Putting yourself out there can be hard! But it can also be really good. If you're the one kid who walks into the room, and you're meeting a new schoolteacher, and you say, "Hi, I'm (fill in the blank) and I'm so excited to be joining your

# What makes you YOU?

What are four things that make you who you are (unique, special, talented you!)?

classroom this year!" That teacher will probably think, "This kid introduced herself! She was really nice." She'll have a great mindset toward you. Trust me, when I go into meetings and introduce myself or make new friends, it's such a good thing. It's a positive to know how to say hello to new people—and not be afraid to put yourself out there. The worst thing that could happen is that they're not interested—but that almost never does!

I meet new people every day. I meet you guys, my fans, all the time! I meet producers, casting directors, executives—all really cool, successful people! And it's great when I can go into the office of the head of Nickelodeon and say, "Hi, I'm JoJo, and I'm so excited to be working with you guys!" It's really a fun thing! After you introduce yourself and say hello, it's weird—it's like you're friends already. That person who seemed so intimidating before? Now they don't seem scary at all!

## Be prepared.

It's better, when you're going to meet someone, if you know a little about them—what they've done or accomplished. Same goes for activities you're about to try. Say you're going to a new restaurant—know what you're getting yourself

into! Obviously you can't know the whole experience, but you can get a little taste of it online. And then when you show up, nothing will throw you off! *Unless* you go to a haunted house . . . then there will be some surprises.

## Have fun!

It's way more fun to meet someone or watch someone onstage who is clearly enjoying what they're doing. If you're doing something you're not enjoying, you won't be confident, and it'll show.

If you're having fun, trust me—it's going to be so much better!

# 8

# Laffy Taffy

#JoJosJokes

# I LOVE, LOVE, LOVE BEING FUNNY. IT'S MY FAVORITE THING.

**HEY SIWANATORZ!** We've been chatting about some serious stuff, so how about a brief pause for some comic relief? I know a lot of jokes off the top of my head, just because you never know when you might need to lighten the mood. I love, love, love being funny. It's my favorite thing. I like to mess with people (in a nice way). Let me tell you about some of the things that make me laugh . . .

. . . So, one time I went to a creepy haunted house with my dad. For Omaha, Nebraska, this was the real deal. It was scary! Keep in mind I was about eight years old at this point. To me, even the *line* was scary—trust me! So finally we got into the haunted house and there was a room set up to look like a little girl's bedroom. There was scary music and flickering, scary lights—it was crazy! Of course there was a creepy little girl in a nightgown standing there, reaching out toward us. When we walked in, she said, "Do you want to have a sleepover with me?" in this really dark, eerie voice. I was a little scared—but I also saw a way to have fun with it. I was like, "Yeah sure!" and I went over to the bed and started jumping on it! I really just wanted to lighten the mood!

A lot of times with scary things, you might want to mix it up with comedy to keep you from being too frightened.

That haunted house was full of surprises, let me tell you! After the sleepover room, we walked into the next room . . . and this one was kind of set up like a jail. It was a haunted, scary-looking jail with a prisoner and a guard. The prisoner was banging on the jail bars and shouting, "Get me out of here!" And the guard was just going crazy! At a haunted house you're not allowed to touch people—but the guard came right up and touched my dad! I said, "Oh my goodness! You're not allowed to touch people." He was kind of messing with my dad, and we were really freaked out. Then he took off his mask and said, "Hi, Tom!" to my dad. Turns out, it was my friend's older brother! It was hilarious!

Speaking of hilarious: My dad and I have this prank tradition that we like to do. It involves fart spray. So, we have these battles to see who can come up with the more creative way to use the fart spray. So far I'm winning!

Once when my dad was scheduled to come to LA for a visit, he surprised my mom by showing up a few hours earlier than he said

he would. When he arrived at our apartment complex, he texted me to come let him in. So I messed with him—I didn't let him in right away. He kept saying, "JoJo, come on! Hurry up and let me in." Meanwhile, I was busy applying the fart spray to a washcloth. Then I opened the door and stuck my hand out, and shoved the fart-spray-covered washcloth in his face! He was so grossed out! He kept saying, "Oh my gosh, I can't believe this is happening!" It was *hilarious*—definitely one of my better pranks.

Another very funny moment happened in front of a bunch of people at a sleepover. One night, a bunch of friends slept over my house and we decided to make a prank call. But not just any prank call. We called up our rival dance studio in Omaha! I pretended to be a mom who wanted to sign her daughter up for dance classes. I said, "Hi, my name is Brittney, and I'd really like to sign my daughter up for classes; but, unfortunately, since you didn't answer your phone, I'll have to call a different studio."

Turns out . . . the studio had caller ID! The next day a bunch of my friends who went there came up to me and said, "Did you prank our studio?" The owner of the studio had sat everyone down and played my recording to the whole studio! It was crazy! So in a way, they sort of pranked me back.

Okay, so now here's a joke I have for you guys!

Are you wearing any shoes or socks right now?

Yes? If so, keep reading.

Do your shoes have holes in them? Like a ripped hole?

I bet you're gonna say "no . . ."

But wait!

If your shoes don't have holes in them, how did you put your feet in?! Get it? Because there's a giant hole you put your foot in!

HERE'S ANOTHER ONE OF MY FAVORITE ONES:

"WHY DID THE CHICKEN CROSS THE ROAD?"

TWEET ME YOUR ANSWER! HASHTAG #JOJOSJOKES

# What are your FAVORITE JOKES?

If you can't think of a joke, write down one of
the times you laughed the hardest.

. . . . . . . . . . . . . . . . . . . . . . . . . . . . . . . . . . . . . . . . . . . . . . . . . .

. . . . . . . . . . . . . . . . . . . . . . . . . . . . . . . . . . . . . . . . . . . . . . . . . .

. . . . . . . . . . . . . . . . . . . . . . . . . . . . . . . . . . . . . . . . . . . . . . . . . .

. . . . . . . . . . . . . . . . . . . . . . . . . . . . . . . . . . . . . . . . . . . . . . . . . .

. . . . . . . . . . . . . . . . . . . . . . . . . . . . . . . . . . . . . . . . . . . . . . . . . .

. . . . . . . . . . . . . . . . . . . . . . . . . . . . . . . . . . . . . . . . . . . . . . . . . .

. . . . . . . . . . . . . . . . . . . . . . . . . . . . . . . . . . . . . . . . . . . . . . . . . .

. . . . . . . . . . . . . . . . . . . . . . . . . . . . . . . . . . . . . . . . . . . . . . . . . .

. . . . . . . . . . . . . . . . . . . . . . . . . . . . . . . . . . . . . . . . . . . . . . . . . .

# 9
## Sour Patch Kids
### #PeaceOutHaterz

# IF YOU'VE EVER BEEN BULLIED ONLINE, YOU UNDERSTAND!

**ONE DAY A COUPLE OF WEEKS** after *Abby's Ultimate Dance Competition* aired, I came downstairs with my phone in my hand, crying. I'd just looked at Abby Lee Miller's Instagram—she'd posted the question, "Who do you want to go home next week?" And dozens of comments said ME! It hurt so bad. I didn't understand why everyone wanted to see me go!

Some people had written nice stuff too, saying how I was their favorite part of the show. But I barely noticed those. All I could see was my name and the reasons that followed. If you've ever been bullied online, you understand!

People wrote horrible things.

They made fun of every part of me, and not just the dancing. They made fun of the way I dressed and looked and even talked. I'd faced down tough judges, heard hard critiques, and gone through elimination. But this felt different. This hurt *way* worse.

# Go troll someone you know . . . in a GOOD WAY!

- Tell someone you like their outfit, or write it on their social media

- Write a note for your best friend, recounting a favorite memory

- Reach out to your favorite author to say why you like their book

Overall, I love social media. Bet most of you Siwanatorz feel the same way! Twitter, Facebook, Musical.ly, YouTube, Snapchat, all of it. Social media is such a fun way to keep in touch with everyone and express yourself—scrolling around on it is one of my favorite things to do in my down time. But along with the good comes the bad.

The day I saw Abby's Instagram post, my mom said to me, "JoJo, why aren't you worried about the people who love you? Why are you worried about the few who want you to go home?"

"They hate me!" I said. "Why do they hate me?"

"Because they're haters," said my mom. "They hide behind a keyboard and don't even leave their name. What they say is meaningless. What matters is how you feel about yourself."

I knew I was a good dancer, no matter what people said. I was also a good friend. I made people laugh, so I must be pretty funny, and I'm always the first one to hug someone who is sad. Sometimes I could act a little silly . . . but that's what made me who I was. I liked that part of myself. I also have good fashion sense. And I *loved* my bows. I'd been wearing them since I was two

years old, and they were just a part of who I was. Why dress like everyone else?

Most important, though, I was a happy kid—I always have been. For me, that was the moment I realized that I could use social media either for good or for bad. I realized the Internet had the power to hurt people in real life . . . or to help them. And I wanted to use my own social media to make people feel good about themselves.

After my tears dried that day, I made a decision. Those words hurt me, and I never wanted anyone to feel that way, if I could help it. Lots of people get bullied. It happens at school and on the Internet every day. Bet it's happened to a lot of you! Some girl is jealous, so she makes up lies . . . or some guy makes a comment about how you look. Comments on the Internet are like gossip at school, only even worse, because it's out there for the world to see.

The fact is, when people want to be mean,
they will be—often for no reason other than
to make themselves feel better.

There was no way I could stop the haters. I knew I wanted to do something, but what? I was just some girl from Nebraska. But after a while, something occurred to me. If I could make people talk online . . . I could potentially make it positive. I made the decision then: I would use my social media to be positive and inspire people. Though I wouldn't put it into action for a long time, that

# Form a CLUB!

What's your club name? What are the rules?
Secret password? Write them down below!

. . . . . . . . . . . . . . . . . . . . . . . . . . . . . . . . . . . . . . . . . . . . . .

. . . . . . . . . . . . . . . . . . . . . . . . . . . . . . . . . . . . . . . . . . . . . .

. . . . . . . . . . . . . . . . . . . . . . . . . . . . . . . . . . . . . . . . . . . . . .

. . . . . . . . . . . . . . . . . . . . . . . . . . . . . . . . . . . . . . . . . . . . . .

. . . . . . . . . . . . . . . . . . . . . . . . . . . . . . . . . . . . . . . . . . . . . .

. . . . . . . . . . . . . . . . . . . . . . . . . . . . . . . . . . . . . . . . . . . . . .

. . . . . . . . . . . . . . . . . . . . . . . . . . . . . . . . . . . . . . . . . . . . . .

. . . . . . . . . . . . . . . . . . . . . . . . . . . . . . . . . . . . . . . . . . . . . .

. . . . . . . . . . . . . . . . . . . . . . . . . . . . . . . . . . . . . . . . . . . . . .

day something important happened: I started wanting to make a difference.

Back then, I was thinking how there must be lots of girls like me. How maybe, one day, I could find them. But I wasn't sure how to make that happen, or if it would work. A lot of people knew who I was from *AUDC*, but not like now. *Dance Moms* would change everything! In that moment, #Siwanatorz was barely an idea.

Now, five years later, we're an army!

In that time, I've blocked and deleted a lot of hate. The more successful you are, the more the haterz will hate. There are a ton out there, and I can't tell you all the mean stuff they've said about me.

No, really. *I can't.* Wanna know why?

I don't care about it! I block it out.

Online haterz are always going to be around, but they need food to survive. Paying attention is like taking them to the all-you-can-eat buffet!

Instead, I focus on the people whose
opinions matter to me: my Siwanatorz!

Sure, not all bullies hide . . . some are right out there in your face. In the past five years, I've faced those kinds too.

If you've ever been a kid, no doubt you know exactly what I mean about in-your-face bullies. I'm talking about that guy in school who threatens people for no reason, or those mean girls who give side-eyes and whisper behind their hands. Maybe they're insecure, or jealous, or just plain old jerks. But whatever the reason, they love making other people feel bad! But here's something I've learned: Unless those people make some major changes, they grow up to be unhappy.

Bullies aren't powerful forever. And those "losers" getting made fun of? They're complex people just like you, with passions and hobbies and dreams and, most importantly, feelings. They have potential to make the world a better place too! *Everyone* has the potential to make the world a better place, if they're kind.

Bullies are scary. Trust me, I know. They like to point out your "flaws," but know what's funny? Sometimes those aren't flaws at all, but the best parts of you! Maybe you are kind of nerdy . . . but that just means you're smart, and everyone knows smart is cool. Or maybe you do have a big personality and talk a lot. But that big personality is what draws people to you . . . and maybe even gets you on TV!

I'm different, but I've learned over time that being different is a good thing. I bet you're different in a good way too. And anyone who doesn't like it, well . . . I've only got one thing to say:

#PeaceOutHaterz

# What makes you different?

Name three things unique to you (a birthmark,
a talent, or whatever makes you stand out!).

. . . . . . . . . . . . . . . . . . . .

. . . . . . . . . . . . . . . . . . . . .

. . . . . . . . . . . . . . . . . . .

# JoJo's Guide
## to
## Standing Up
## to the Hate

# Build a wall.

When I tell people to build a wall, I don't physically mean, "Get the bricks, get the glue, get the cement, get the paint" to build a wall. I mean, *be able to build an imaginary wall*. If there's a bully or a hater in front of you and they're saying something rude, build an imaginary wall, so it can't get through. If it's a big cement wall, you're not going to be able to hear what they're saying. Just say, "Okay, I'm going to go hang out with my friends now." Don't let the bullies knock you down. Be yourself and have fun with your life.

## Be kind.

Although it can be hard to be kind when someone's being mean, you have to understand that you can't fight fire with fire. What I mean by that is, if you have a fire, you need to put water—the opposite—on it. If there's a bully and they're being mean, put in kindness—the opposite of cruelty. Selena Gomez wrote one of my favorite songs, "Kill Them with Kindness." What she's talking about in that song is stepping up and being extra kind if someone's not being very nice. Like my mom always says, "Take the high road!"

## Hold the drama.

Girls are sometimes mean. Trust me, I know. I've had to deal with it before. But for every mean girl, there are a dozen other girls who are really nice and fun to hang out with. That's why you can't get too caught up in the highs and lows. There are *always* highs and lows—no matter what or who your friends are. No matter what, hold the drama. Focus on what's important. And if you're like me, just dance. *Dance dance dance dance dance dance.*

## Turn sour to sweet.

No matter what happens in life, there's always a silver lining. You don't always know what the positive is going to be right away; but if you keep your eyes and mind open, you will find it.

## Talk to others.

If there is a bully or a hater or someone who's not nice, do something about it! Go to an adult—a principal, parent, teacher, or friend. If something is hurting you or someone else, be brave and ask people for help! You might be afraid it will make the bullying worse—but bullies count on your fear and silence. If you speak up to the right trusted person, not only will you have someone on your side to help stop the bullying but you'll also break the hold the bully has over you. And often bullies turn out to be the most frightened people of all. I always turn to my mom for help, and she always gets me through it.

# 10

# Good & Plenty

# FriendsAreEverywhere

# WHEN I GO HOME, I LOVE HAVING PARTIES AND SLEEPOVERS WITH EVERYONE.

**REMEMBER HOW I SAID I BECAME FRIENDS** with a lot of the off-camera people at *AUDC*? No one was more surprised than I was when friends just sort of snuck up on me. The same is true for me everywhere! I've always had a lot of friends from dance, both in Nebraska and California. In Nebraska we had a code word for our little group of dance friends: Batman! We all had Batman T-shirts and met in an alley in a black Suburban and swapped secrets. I'm still so close with that group, and all my friends from home! When I go home, I love having parties and sleepovers with everyone. My friends and I have our own version of Monopoly, where we make our own secret rules—and we even make special money.

Leaving my Omaha friends to move to California was very, very hard. When I first started to grow on social media and to be on TV, some of my friends got really jealous and were mean to me. On the flip side, some got really excited and happy for me. When something happens to set you apart—when a change pushes you somewhere your friends aren't—there's going to be a little stress on those relationships. This will happen even if you're just no longer next-door neighbors, or no longer in the same school! Any kind of change is hard on friendships. You know your friends are jealous if you ask them to hang out and they go, "No, sorry," for no reason. You know if you're really nice to them and they're not nice to you anymore,

that they're no longer your friend. And if someone's trying to use you . . . that person is definitely not a real friend. Luckily, most of my old friends were proud of me when big things started happening with my career, and we're still really close.

Now I have a lot of new friends in addition to the old ones who got through the changes with me. Most of my new friends are really great— but some of them want to be my friend just *because* of the TV stuff.

And that's weird too. I have to be careful, and learn to read people, and not get too upset when they disappoint me. But I always assume the best—if you don't, that's not good either! I try to stay positive no matter what, and to give everyone the benefit of the doubt.

When I moved out to LA, I became friends with a lot of people who don't "make sense" in an obvious way. I've always been able to

MY OLD FRIENDS WERE PROUD OF ME WHEN BIG THINGS STARTED HAPPENING WITH MY CAREER, AND WE'RE STILL REALLY CLOSE.

carry on a conversation with anyone—it's a skill I'm really proud of. I can hang out with five-year-olds and have fun, or with forty-year-olds and have fun. Friends come in unlikely shapes and sizes. If you go into a situation saying, "I'm only going to be friends with so-and-so," you're going to miss out on a lot of amazing people.

Now that I live in LA, I have all kinds of friends! Some are younger than I am and some are older. Some teach me new things, and others I am able to inspire.

Recently I met Gwen Stefani—she was amazing! I've met Meghan Trainor and Mario Lopez. I love being able to hang out with people who are successful in their own careers, and learn from them too. I'm not intimidated by the age difference—I just see it as an opportunity to grow. A lot of my friends are either younger than I am by a few years, or much older. Since a lot of my friends are YouTubers, they get all the references I get. And if the older ones start talking about stuff that happened when they were kids—let's say they're singing "Girls Just Want to Have Fun" by Cyndi Lauper—I know it too, because I love the 1980s! My theory is that I was actually born in the eighties and the government transplanted me to present day. Just check out the way I dress if you need proof.

When I was home in Nebraska for the Halo Awards, some of my favorite California friends flew out for my Halo party to surprise me. I was so happy, I cried! It was Rebecca and Josh, and Rebecca's

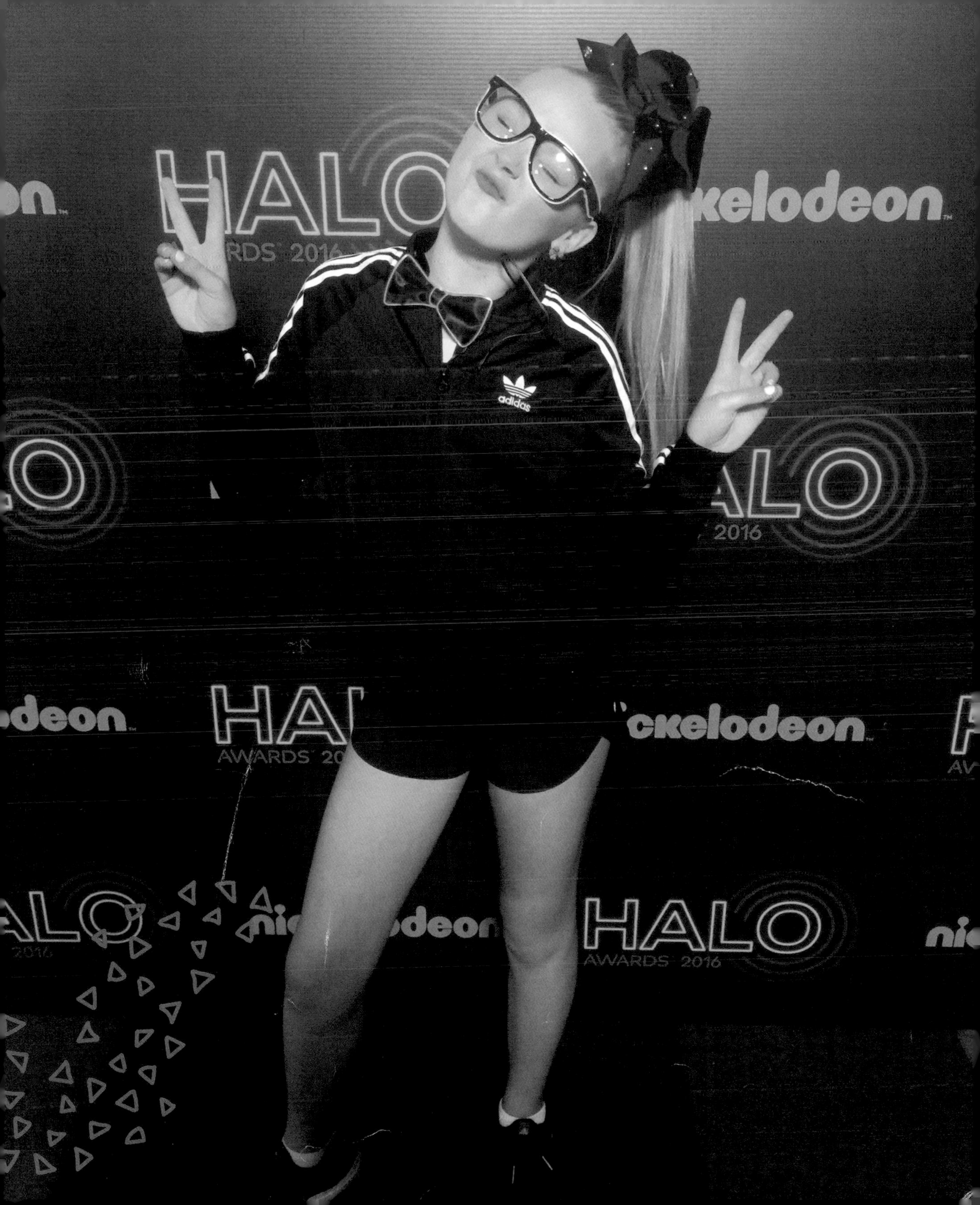
HALO
AWARDS 2016
adidas

...A LOT OF FRIENDSHIPS CAN SURPRISE YOU. SOMETIMES THEY COME EASY—BUT SOMETIMES PEOPLE JUST TAKE TIME TO WARM UP.

husband, Matt. When I first met them, we were all hanging out in the greenroom at the YouTube event and started talking, and then I kept running into them at other events. Eventually they asked me how they could help with my YouTube channel. They taught me which software to get, and showed me the basics of photo editing. They were so nice and supportive! And then we started collaborating, and now we're all good friends. When they came to Nebraska, it was amazing—it meant so much to me to have my California and Omaha friends together, hanging out and celebrating.

The funny thing is, a lot of friendships can surprise you. Sometimes they come easy—but sometimes people just take time to warm up. By the time I left *Dance Moms*, I'd made so many friendships—and I didn't want to leave anyone behind. I begged my mom to go back so we could say goodbye to everyone. We all still talk constantly, Snapchat, and stay in touch. I'm not talking about just the girls—they were amazing, but there were a lot of other friendships happening off-screen: crew, makeup, camera people, producers.

I always keep my eyes open, and I always give everyone a chance—no matter what their situation. You never know who will walk into your life and change it forever!

# JOJO'S GUIDE TO MAKING FRIENDS

# Give the kindness you want to receive.

If you want really good friends, you've got to *be* a really good friend! Same goes for attracting good people into your life in the first place—if you put kindness out there, you're more likely to get it back. Remember my friend Josh? My unexpected friend? That's one thing he's all about: *Just be nice.* Here are some ideas for ways you can spread the love:

- Tell someone you like their hair

- Tell someone you like their outfit

- Tell someone "good job" in dance, athletics, or whatever activity they're doing

- Encourage someone: Say, "You must be working really hard!"

- Invite someone over to your house, especially if they don't get to hang out a lot with other kids at school

- Hold a door open for an elderly person

- Help someone who's having trouble with their homework

- If you have a little extra, donate food or clothes to charity

- . . . . . . . . . . . . . . . . . . . . . . . . . . . . . . . . . . . . . .

- . . . . . . . . . . . . . . . . . . . . . . . . . . . . . . . . . . . . . .

- . . . . . . . . . . . . . . . . . . . . . . . . . . . . . . . . . . . . . .

- . . . . . . . . . . . . . . . . . . . . . . . . . . . . . . . . . . . . . .

- . . . . . . . . . . . . . . . . . . . . . . . . . . . . . . . . . . . . . .

*I left five blank spots for you to fill in with your ideas! Write them down, then tweet me your favorite! #WorkHardPlayNice*

## Don't be shy.

Believe in yourself! You're a fun person—friends are fun and you're fun, so it's all a perfect match. Sure, sometimes you might meet someone and it's not gonna work out, but other times you might meet someone and you click immediately and realize they're your new best friend! Try

. . . friends are fun and you're fun, so it's all a perfect match.

not to be afraid to go out into the world and say, "Hi, I'm (fill in the blank), who wants to be my friend?" Trust me, I've done that before, and it's paid off!

## Invite someone over.

If there's a new kid in school, invite them over to your house for a pizza party! If you're just joining a sports team and you don't know who to be friends with, ask someone to come over after practice! Nothing's ever wrong with asking—what's the worst they can say? No? For every one person who says "no," I bet you ten will say "yes"— it's worth the risk! Invite someone out for ice cream with you and your mom, or to come over and hang out, or to rehearse together. Odds are they'll say, "Yeah, let's do it, it'll be fun!"

## Pay attention.

Listen to what your friends are saying. Your friends are only there to help you! They're not going to tell you, "You should get a new hairdo" if they don't think that! Your friends are there for you. On the flip side, you have to know what's important to your friends! If you want them to throw you a surprise party for your birthday, make sure you know when *their* birthday is. You've gotta do it first! Make sure you're a thoughtful friend. Ask questions about your friends' lives. Who's into watching a Harry Potter marathon? Who's getting new headshots that weekend? Knowing what's going on with them—and most of all, listening—will show you care.

## Don't get jealous.

Believe me, it's hard when a friend does something really cool, and you think, "I wish I could do that!" But you can't get jealous! There's a difference between jealousy and wishing and hoping. If you're jealous, it's not very nice. And there's no point! Be happy for your friends and excited they're doing something cool! Be excited for them that they're going on a new adventure! Ask them to send you pictures! There's room for everyone to do great things!

## Be happy for your friends and excited they're doing something cool!

# 11

# Kinder Surprise

#CalmCoolCollected

# THE CALL THAT CHANGED MY LIFE CAME ON A SATURDAY.

**"JOJO," SAID SCOTT,** the executive field producer from *Dance Moms*, "we want you on the show!" I went crazy! One of the producers liked me from *AUDC* and had brought me out to Florida to audition for *Dance Moms*, one of the top-rated shows on television, with an even bigger viewership than *AUDC*! But then time went by and . . . nothing. During that time, my life was on hold—I knew I might be on the show, but didn't know if they'd need me for sure, or when. Then one random day during a dance competition, Scott made the call.

I was going to be on *Dance Moms*! And it was going to happen . . . soon.

Really, really soon!

"Oh my gosh," I said, after I finally calmed down. "Did they say . . . ?"

"Yes," said my mom, looking as shocked as I felt. "They want you to start Monday."

It was Saturday.

We were away at a dance convention all weekend, and on Monday, we had to go to Pittsburgh for a week! They said to us, "Bring bows! Be yourselves. Be entertaining."

You know how people say, "Everything changed overnight"? Well, in my case, that was 100 percent true. There was hardly time to say goodbye to my friends, or even pack my stuff. I was going to be on *Dance Moms* in . . . *two days!* Would I be ready in time?

*Are you kidding?* I'd been ready my whole life!

But only having two days, there wasn't too much time to feel sad. Just excited . . . and busy! My mom and I flew to Pittsburgh two days later. It took until I was in the airport for reality to sink in. When it was time to say goodbye to my brother and dad, it finally hit me. I was leaving . . . and they were staying behind.

Being on *Dance Moms* was my ultimate goal—even bigger than being on *AUDC*. And with *AUDC*, we knew we'd only be gone for a month at most. With *Dance Moms*, nothing was certain, but we hoped to be gone for even longer than that, if things went well. My dad and Jayden supported me as always, but they couldn't leave their whole lives behind to come with us. It was scary, not knowing how long we'd be apart. My brother had a baseball team depending on him, and a ton of friends. My dad had all his patients. He's a chiropractor, which is a kind of doctor who deals mostly with back pain. His patients depend on him. He makes people feel better for a living! When we said goodbye, he did the same for me.

When we arrived, I was so nervous! We were about to walk into

# What is standing in YOUR path?

What are three things standing in your path,
and how can you crush them?

# Dance Moms POP QUIZ!

1. Where was the original Abby Lee Dance Company located?. . . . . . . . . . . . . . . . . . . . .

2. What was Mackenzie's first name before it was changed to Mackenzie? . . . . . . . . . . . . . .

3. What is JoJo's natural hair color?. . . . . . . . . . . . . . . . . .

4. What is the name of Kendall's cat?. . . . . . . . . . . . . . . .

5. What was the original name of the show? . . . . . . . . . . . . . . . . . . . . . . . . . . . .

Answers: 1. Pittsburgh. 2. Taylor. 3. Brown. 4. Rebel. 5. Just Dance.

the famous Abby Lee Dance Company studio! The producers gave us a call time and told us to wait in the car—they were going to come get us. We wound up waiting for two hours before they said it was our turn. Then we sat in the lobby for another hour before we could finally go in. By then, though, I was used to waiting.

Finally, we went into the studio—and they told us I'd get a solo and a group dance! I was going to appear on the show, but I wasn't a full member of the cast yet. This was more of an audition, the producer explained, and for the time being I was a guest. If it went well, maybe I'd make the team and be a regular on *Dance Moms*. Then again, I could be headed home in just a few days!

This was my chance. I knew if I did really, really well I had a chance to become a permanent member of the cast. But I also knew it wasn't a sure thing— the pressure was on.

By the time I stepped into the *Dance Moms* world, it had already been around for a while. It was 2014 when I came along, and the show was in Season 4. Most of the girls had been around since the beginning. Nia, Maddie, and Mackenzie started in 2011, when *Dance Moms* first aired. They pretty much grew up on the show, and so did Kendall, who started in Season 2. The only newcomer was Kalani, who had been on for a year and a half and was officially part of the team.

Then there was me. The new girl.

I was a last-minute replacement for someone who left the show suddenly. By the time I arrived, it was already episode three of the new season, and the other girls were still in shock at having lost their teammate and friend. It's never easy being the new girl, especially when you're replacing someone else who everyone knew and loved. It takes time! In the early days, I never knew for sure if I'd have someone to sit with on the travel buses, when we went to competitions. I missed my friends from home and wasn't immediately best friends with the *Dance Moms* girls—it takes time!

But I showed up every day with a big smile, and I was my best, nicest self. And pretty soon, the other girls felt a lot better about having me around! Sometimes it takes weeks or even months to get close to new friends—but once you do, it's so worth it. I always knew I was a fun, caring, good friend with lots to give. I was confident the other girls would love me once they got to know me—I just had to be myself. And I was right! Once the rest of the cast realized my mom and I were in it for the long haul, they accepted us—and over time, they became a second family. Soon they started greeting me with hugs every day, saying, "We're so glad you're here!"

So here's a little *Dance Moms* secret: For every hour-long show, they film literally *hundreds* of hours! Imagine if they made a show about your life, and you'll understand. What do you do on the average day? Brush your teeth, text your BFF, study for a quiz, go to soccer practice . . . and during all that, a few cool things might happen. Maybe you get the highest grade or make a sick goal during a game or get a couple thousand likes on one of your Instagram posts!! That stuff is interesting, but the rest . . . *not as much*. To the person living it, it might be interesting . . . but not to TV audiences around the world.

The same was true with us! For every exciting moment you see—like Pyramid, where we get ranked according to performance, or performing in competition—there was a lot of other stuff that would bore you to tears! I mean, who wants to watch me practice the same dance move a hundred times until I get it right? Or watch us eat lunch, try on costumes, and spend hours learning a routine? Like I said, everything is real, but it's only a small slice of our lives. And to get the good stuff, they have to film *a lot*. In other words, we practically lived at the studio! It wasn't easy, that's for sure.

It's crazy to be on a set on a show you've watched for years. When we first arrived, my mom and I had one week to prove ourselves!

I danced my heart out, and my mom made her mark too—even the producer said so. My mom and I were basically a dream team that week. We were supposed to stay for seven days . . . and we wound up staying for two and a half seasons and over one hundred episodes.

On TV, there are about fifty people behind the scenes that nobody ever sees. In addition to the cast, we were close with all of the crew too! During those days of filming in Pittsburgh, hanging out with our huge new TV "family" quickly became the new norm. Later, when Abby opened a second studio in Los Angeles and the show began filming there, we stayed just as tight. We'd film all day long then go to the Grove at night—that's a shopping center in Los Angeles with amazing food and stores— and then hang out at Melissa's apartment afterward. (Melissa is Maddie and Mackenzie's mom.) We'd even carpool to school with all the dance moms. No matter whose car we were in we'd listen to music and jam, but all the girls liked my mom's car the best! The other moms were fun—they weren't super 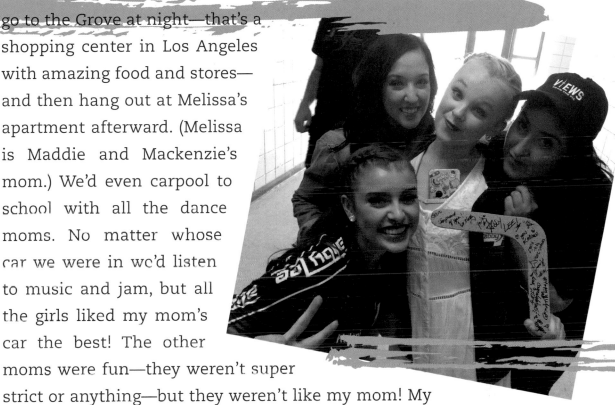 strict or anything—but they weren't like my mom! My mom would say, "Girls, let's take the long way to school!" And she'd play all the music we wanted to listen to.

During *Dance Moms*, we had such an adventure. We saw the world—so many cities and states, and even Australia! We were there for three weeks! I loved my *Dance Moms* family. It was an amazing time. There were ups and downs like there are with anything in life, but it was almost always fun! Friday nights when the moms all went to dinner and shopping, we girls would hang out in Maddie and Mackenzie's room because it was the biggest. We'd have pizza parties and give each other massages and have ugly dance-offs and

OUR MOMS USED TO TALK ABOUT HOW LUCKY THEY WERE TO HAVE THE NICEST KIDS.

talk and laugh all night. Everyone wanted to get along, and so we did. No matter how tired or stressed we were, we all made that extra effort to be good. We'd even agree on what food to order! Our moms used to talk about how lucky they were to have the nicest kids.

We filmed Tuesday through Saturday, and each day had a specific purpose: Tuesday was interview day. Each interview took about two hours! Wednesday was Pyramid. Thursdays we had rehearsal. Friday we had rehearsal in the morning, then traveled to wherever our competition was that weekend. Then Saturday, of course, was competition day! During the week we worked every day from about 8 A.M., which is when we started school, until about 5 P.M. They were long days, and it was intense.

The travel buses were usually really gross, but there was always a big Tupperware full of snacks. Mackenzie and I would charge people a dollar for a massage. And we'd always make at least one stop anywhere Abby wanted. I remember the very first time we went on the bus: My mom and I saw that all the other girls had MacBooks—but I didn't. When I got my first paycheck for the show, though, we made a trip to Best Buy—it was a reward for all my hard work!

It was a lot of fun working with Abby—she had a big personality and knew so much about dance, and about Broadway. Actually, Abby knew everything about everything! She was full of facts—anything you brought up, she could weigh in with new information. She even told us once the real reason why Michael Jackson always wore a glove on one hand. (Google it! It's a really cool story!)

# JOJO'S GUIDE TO HANDLING SURPRISES

# Go with it.

If you're in a situation where you have to leave all your friends, or something bad happens and your life changes— I'm not going to sugarcoat it—it will be hard. But always know it will eventually turn out okay. Rolling with the punches isn't easy for anyone, but you get used to it! One of the things that helped me deal was looking for positives in my life. In my case, that was my relationship with my mom—she was always there with me, no matter what the challenge. Knowing I could count on her, I could relax and move forward—even on the hard days.

# Change won't last forever.

At first, if you move schools or experience some other big change, it's going to be hard, 100 percent. But just know there's a rainbow at the end of the tunnel. Most people say there's a light, but I say a rainbow, because it's more fun. Sometimes you have to look pretty hard for the rainbow, but you just have to trust that it'll be there. And in the meantime, lean on the people you love. If you feel like you don't have someone there for you, I'm there for you! And so is every Siwanator. Tweet at @itsjojosiwa #JoJosGuide and tag your best friend!

## Know your squad.

Right now I'm very lucky because I have a lot of people in my life I can count on. I have my family, I have my friends, and I have my pets! You might be thinking, "Crazy, pets," but hey! They love me unconditionally, and I love them— they're my favorites! Even if it's hard to find your people, always know there's a squad out there somewhere waiting to be found. And in the meantime, like I said above—you have me, and you have the Siwanatorz!

So reach out on social media! Use the Siwanatorz hashtag—even if I can't respond, someone else will! Wear your favorite bow so other Siwanatorz can spot you. And when you see another Siwanator, give them a big smile.

## We're all in this together!

# Name your CREW!

What are the names of the people you're closest to?
Now list the first letters in a row, and write a trait
they each have, beginning with that letter.

*Example:*

| A | for Anna who is Artistic.

[ ] for _____ who is _____ .

[ ] for _____ who is _____ .

[ ] for _____ who is _____ .

[ ] for _____ who is _____ .

[ ] for _____ who is _____ .

[ ] for _____ who is _____ .

# 12

# Gobstopper

#CantStopWontStop

# NOT TOO LONG AFTER DANCE MOMS CAME ANOTHER LIFE-CHANGING MOMENT.

**WHEN I WAS ELEVEN AND PERFORMING** in Las Vegas, a woman named Caryn had come out to see me dance. She was looking for a social media influencer to pair with her business, and she thought I might be a great fit. She met me backstage and asked me a bunch of questions about what I wanted—so I told her about my dream of becoming a pop star. She said to me, "JoJo, you're going to be famous."

Even though we'd just met, I could tell Caryn believed in my talent. I liked her right away, and she and my mom totally hit it off too! A couple of weeks later, Caryn became my manager. Now she and my mom and I are a dream team—best friends who get things done! My life was already exciting—but after I met Caryn, so many cool things started happening. Caryn had a vision for me—and it was perfect. It was exactly what I'd always wanted for myself. Best of all, she knew how to help me get there.

Not long after Caryn and I started working together, my bows became big. Well . . . they were already BIG—literally! But when I'd wear them, people would stop me and ask, "Where did you get that amazing bow?" My bows were getting attention even from people who didn't know me from *Dance Moms!* We knew a good opportunity when we saw it . . . and so did Claire's, a major accessories line across the United States. Soon my bows were being sold everywhere! Working with Claire's was incredible! I did photo shoots for them, sometimes even with my dog, BowBow. I've loved every minute of working with Claire's. Life was amazing.

## But it was about to get even better.

I had never forgotten what happened that day on Abby's Instagram—the day I realized how powerful social media could be, for good or for bad. And I still thought a lot about what had happened with Lucy in the third grade, when we were making our ice cream sundaes. Everyone gets bullied sometimes, I'd realized. There wasn't a kid out there who didn't know what it felt like. I'd wanted to do something *bigger* for a long time. But for a long time, I didn't know what that would be. Suddenly, *I had it.* I could work on making my own dreams come true while also doing what was most important to me: making girls feel *powerful.*

You know what I'm getting at—one word: *Boomerang!*

Making "Boomerang" was amazing. I always knew I wanted to write songs, and I knew I wanted my songs to be inspiring. Then

one day it hit me: A boomerang comes back, just like people can bounce back against the hate—bigger, better, faster, and stronger.

Maybe a creative thing you can do is to think about all the *nice* people in your life and write them notes! It could be anything really—but I'm a big believer in taking the bad stuff that's thrown at you and turning it into new, amazing, impossibly cool stuff.

"Boomerang" means a lot to me—it isn't just a song. It's a way for me—and every girl—to be strong against bullies. If someone says the word *boomerang*, I automatically think of anti-bullying. It's all about how haters keep talking their talk, but I can keep walking my walk—they can't get to me.

I wrote the song with three other writers when I was twelve. I'd throw out ideas, and they'd help switch around the words. It was so fun writing it—so cool to hear all the different versions! One early version had a tambourine in it and went, "boom, boom aaaay." It was so crazy to see how it changed! I *loved* how it turned out.

Making "Boomerang" wasn't all easy, though. Everything you do has challenges! But you just have to be strong. There were tough days when I wasn't as confident about my singing. When I had to do the "ohh, ohh, woah ahh"—that part was hard for me! I wasn't as sure of my voice then—I wish I'd been more confident! But I learned so much from the challenge. I recorded "Boomerang" into the same microphone Christina Aguilera sang "Genie in a Bottle" into! Talk about inspiring!

Recording the video was *so* much fun! My hair and makeup artist, Diana, owns a production company called BluBot Studios. They shot the video; but first we had to figure out what we wanted it to look like! We met up with BluBot and all came up with a storyboard together—that's when you map out the story you want to tell, and what you want it to look like. Then we filmed the video.

Best part of all? Every friend I had from Nebraska, Iowa, California—practically everyone I knew—was in the video!

I wanted to be surrounded by my friends. My very best friend from Omaha, Halle, played my best friend in the video. EJ played the shy girl. My other good friend, Sydney, played the other BFF. Every single person in the video was somebody I knew! It was so amazing to be surrounded by my best friends in the world while singing about how to stand up to the bullies *together*.

We shot from 8 A.M. until 1 A.M. the next day at Oaks Christian School here in California. Since all my friends were there, it was super fun, like an all-day party! There are so many secret, cool things hidden inside "Boomerang"— if you watch the video you'll find them! But I'll give you a couple of clues to start. One of the secrets is that there's a license plate on the wall in the hallway of the school—it was supposed to be on the car, and we didn't like it because it had a lowercase j in JoJo. So we got a new one and it was absolutely perfect!

BowBow was even in the video! She was so little back then that she could fit in my brother's hoodie pocket! Kendall, my friend from *Dance Moms*, was the lead mean girl. We rehearsed everything at Abby's studio in LA. Then BluBot edited it and added animation.

After months of hard work, I got to see the final version of the video, and it was so good!!! It was everything I wanted it to be! When it aired on May 17, 2016, I was nervous. I didn't know if fans

were gonna like it or be obsessed with it like I was! But it wasn't even really about how popular it would be—it was just something I wanted to do to get my message out there.

So I posted it to my YouTube channel for everyone to see . . . and the response from all my fans was incredible! When it first came out, it got two million views per day! Now, more than a year later, it gets 500,000 views per day, which is amazing!!!! It just goes to show how many people need to feel powerful when bullies are trying to break them down. Now it has hundreds of millions of views, which is unbelievable, and so awesome! I feel very lucky that my song has reached so many people. Little kids as young as four years old come up to me and say, "Are you the 'Boomerang' girl?" It's so fun to see the little kids that love it so much. And I hope they grow up feeling powerful and ready for anything because of that song!

Things after that got pretty crazy very fast.

After the experience with "Boomerang," I knew I wanted to form a supportive group for kids who stick together, especially when someone is being bullied.

I officially created the Siwanatorz, and you guys were amazing from the start—tweeting, commenting, and being kind to one another. Pretty soon after that, I flew out to New York to meet with book publishers about *JoJo's Guide to the Sweet Life*, which I hope will give you some tips for dealing with haterz and living an awesome life. I signed an overall talent deal with Nickelodeon . . . and I won a Kids' Choice Award! Everything I'd ever dreamed about was starting to come true, and fast. Suddenly I had to work harder than ever . . . but it was exactly what I'd always wanted, and so much fun.

One day not too long ago, I got a call from the *New York Times*. They wanted to do a feature on me for the Style section! My mom and I were so surprised and excited! And then they told me I was going to

●●○○ Sprint 📶     3:58 AM     44% 🔋

Photo

heraccny

Liked by **okitzjojo**, **ziegxsiwa** and **1,943 others**

**heraccny** FRONT PAGE FASHION ALERT! So excited to be featured in today's style section of @nytimes! #linkinbio

View all 66 comments

be on the *cover* of the Style section. *The cover of the* New York Times *Style section.* I couldn't believe it!

The reporter from the *Times* called and interviewed me at the Nickelodeon Kids' Choice Awards. They asked me all about my bows and my Nickelodeon deal, and why I think the bows are so popular. Then, a couple of weeks later when we were in Nebraska, they called and said they wanted to set up a photo shoot! They sent a photographer to my home in Omaha, and they took photos of me with my bows in my bedroom, living room, and by my piano. They even took some of BowBow! It wasn't my first time doing a shoot for a magazine, but I'd never done anything as big as the *New York Times*. It was a huge deal. We talked about why my bows are so big—how it's the positive messaging behind it that makes my bows different from everyone else's. They're a cute, giant, adorable hair accessory—but at the same time, there's a message about being kind to others and standing up for yourself. I tell everyone, if you're wearing a JoJo bow or see someone wearing one, you know automatically that they're kind! It's like spotting members of a secret club—you see someone and you know you have something in common. Seeing my *Times* profile was one of the best moments of my life.

At the time, it felt like life couldn't get any better! But now I know I'm only just getting started . . .

# JOJO'S GUIDE
## TO LIVING YOUR
### BEST LIFE

# Bounce back.

You all know the words . . . sing it, Siwanatorz!

> I don't really care about what they say
> I'ma come back like a boomerang
> Won't let the haterz get their way
> I'ma come back like a boomerang

Guys, this isn't just some catchy song I made up . . . it seriously works! Bouncing back is maybe the most important thing when people get you down. *You* decide whether you bounce back. *You* decide what happens next. When you think like that, it takes away all the power from the bullies. They might want to keep you down—but why let them win when you can bounce back?

# Be creative.

Put all your energy into something BIG! Why not make up a song or a dance, or paint a really cool piece of art and post it online? Chances are there's someone out there

# Make up your own song!

Either the lyrics or the music or both!
Write your lyrics below.

....................................................................

....................................................................

....................................................................

....................................................................

....................................................................

....................................................................

....................................................................

....................................................................

who will love it and support you. You never know what can come from the smallest things! I posted "Boomerang" on my YouTube channel, and it reached millions of people! Even if you touch just one person, it's important. So make something that means something, and reach out!

## You do you, boo.

The only way to live your best life is to be yourself! Don't follow the crowd or do what everyone else is doing because it's cool. Just do what makes you happy! Maybe that's totally weird and you're worried no one will like it—guess what, it's going to make *you* happy!

## And that's what matters! Being different is a good thing—it's your chance to show what makes you special!

# 13

# Starburst

#LuckyCharmedLife

# CAN I JUST SAY THAT I AM OBSESSED WITH NICKELODEON?

**WE'VE TALKED A LOT ABOUT MY CAREER,** but we haven't gone deep into the latest, greatest, and most obvious development: NICKELODEON!

Can I just say that I am obsessed with Nickelodeon?

This past year, I signed an overall talent deal with Nickelodeon. We're doing all kinds of amazing stuff together—books, toys, and my TV show with my Nick friends! All the Nick offices are fun, but I *love* hanging out at the ones in Burbank, California. I go there a lot to work, but it's also playtime! You get there and walk into the lobby and there are big, light-up letters—maybe seven feet tall—that say "Nick." It's so cool! And they have these chairs that are like spinning tops—you sit in them and spin around. And the New York offices are right by the big Viacom monitor in Times Square. You take the elevator up to the Nickelodeon floors, and they have walls you can color on, a ball room, Legos, a Ping-Pong table, and a room of all their merchandise. It's a kid paradise!

# What's YOUR favorite?

What's your favorite character from each of your favorite Nickelodeon shows? Draw a cartoon where they're all hanging out!

Since I signed with Nickelodeon I've guest starred on *School of Rock*; starred on two of their Halloween specials; been on the *Sizzling Summer Camp Special* and the *Not-So-Valentine's Special*; performed at the Halo Awards; guest-starred on *Make It Pop* . . . there are so many things! Every once in a while it hits me, and I think, "Wow! I work for Nickelodeon!!" It's such a great feeling. One of my favorite things is going to their offices and seeing everything that's in the works. I know of future Nick projects that no one else knows about. It's so cool!

## All the Nick friends are like a big family.

When you come in and you're the new kid, you're nervous at first—everyone already has their crew—then six months later, you're in the family. Luckily I'd been through it all before on *Dance Moms*, where it really takes until your second season to be part of the family. Nickelodeon was exactly the same. Now I'm friends with every single cast member in every show. Me and Ricardo from *School of Rock* are really good friends! He was one of the first people who made me feel like I fit in, and I will never forget that—I plan to always do the same for other new people.

The day of the Nickelodeon Kids' Choice Awards, I was so excited. I had no idea if I was about to win or lose, but either way, I knew it was going to be a fun day. Even if I lost and was sad, I knew I'd just get right back up, clap for whoever won, and have a fun night. I had my friends and family there—how could I not?

That day was one of the best days of my life. I remember waking up thinking, "Today's my day! Today I could win an orange blimp!" Around noon, my hair and makeup artist came over and we were talking and having fun. An hour after that, my friends came over: Debbie, Matt, Rebecca, Josh, and my mom and dad. My brother had to stay home in Omaha for baseball, but I missed him like crazy, so we FaceTimed!

We ordered pizza and had cupcakes when I was getting ready. We were all dancing and singing in my apartment! Everyone except

me was all dressed up—I was just hanging out in my sweatpants while I got my hair and makeup done . . . but then it came time for me to put my outfit on. Everyone loved it! It was the world's cutest outfit. I wore a really cool slime jacket—it was neon colors—and an orange skirt. That outfit was my favorite that I've worn to any event.

It meant so much to me to have my friends supporting me that entire day. Finally, back in my apartment, it was time to leave—the car had arrived. I remember saying to everyone, "No matter what, you'll still love me, right?" And of course they told me they would. We were jamming out to Josh and Matt's

# Dream BIG!

List your dreams (like what you want to be when you grow up) or tell about an actual dream you remember!

........................................................

........................................................

........................................................

........................................................

........................................................

........................................................

........................................................

........................................................

........................................................

song, "Man in the Mirror/Love Never Felt So Good" and my song, "Boomerang"—then we got out of the car and it was time to walk the red carpet (which is actually a Nick orange carpet, by the way!). I did tons of press interviews and met so many cool people on the red carpet. Then the show began.

It was a big deal. Win or lose, it was an important day for me. About an hour into the show, it was time for my category. I listened to the announcer say, "And the nominees for favorite viral music artist are . . ." They called all the nominees, and I was one of them. I remember looking at the screen thinking, "Wow, that's me up there— I'm up with these really amazing people!" It was such an honor even to be nominated. Then my friends from *School of Rock* announced the

winner: "JOJO SIWA!" It was awesome! I was so excited, my mind went blank. I walked up to the stage to reccive my award, and there was a camera on me, and all I could think of was how great it was. I was in total shock. I hadn't rehearsed a speech at all—so what poured out in those moments was totally from my heart.

I like to keep it genuine, and looking at it later, I saw how emotional it was for me. I was so in shock in that moment, and in my speech, I said exactly what I was feeling: that I was just a kid from Nebraska who'd followed her dreams.

Afterward, I went backstage and took pictures with the blimp! It was so awesome! The first person that I saw who I knew besides the *School of Rock* cast was my publicist, Kim. She was so happy for me!

# What qualities do you have that make you a STAR?

I wrote a few star-worthy qualities below—add your own!

- Kindness

- Thoughtfulness

- Humor

- Confidence

- . . . . . . . . . . . . . .

- . . . . . . . . . . . . . .

- . . . . . . . . . . . . . .

Then I looked up at my friends who were sitting in the audience—everyone was cheering for me. The whole experience was incredible. After we left the show, we celebrated at Maestro's Steakhouse. It's one of my favorite places, and I was surrounded by people I loved. When I woke up the following morning, it was so great to process it all over again and think about what had happened. It was one of the biggest achievements and best moments of my life and career so far, and I owe that to you guys! If you weren't so awesome and enthusiastic and supportive, I wouldn't be where I am!

My mom says luck is when being prepared meets opportunity. Dream big and work hard and don't let anyone tell you no. I didn't know if people would like "Boomerang" when I wrote it. I did it because it meant something to me. I wrote and danced my heart out. It went viral because everyone can relate to not fitting in; also, being with friends and dancing makes everyone feel good.

My career is still developing, and I have so much ahead of me. Maybe I'll make movies! Maybe I'll write my own screenplay! Maybe I'll be a surgeon. Dance will always be a part of my life. It will always be my first love. But its role in my life is changing. And that's not a bad thing.

Change is never a bad thing. Who knows where
I'll be in ten years? Whatever it is, though,
I'll give it 100 percent. That's me.
And that's you too if you want it to be!

# JOJO'S GUIDE TO BEING SUCCESSFUL

# Work hard.

No joke, I used to train for dance twenty-five hours per week. I knew that's what I had to do to measure up to the girls who had more technical training—so I did it. It was work, but it was fun, you know? I had a studio in my basement that I'd use to practice whenever I wasn't at dance class. Doing what you love really helps—it feels less like work and more like playtime! When you hold your dreams in sight, work is just a way to get the life you want!

# Take chances.

Sometimes when you're working at something, you might fall into a routine . . . but you've gotta take crazy chances, and you've gotta go explore the world, because how else will you come up with the next crazy thing? For me, I love trying new things. Some people don't. If you don't, that's totally fine too. But at the same time—trust me when I say this—you'll almost never regret trying something new!

The thing could be really small. If you like smooth peanut butter, try crunchy peanut butter! Who knows, it could change your life.

## Be patient.

Dreams don't come true overnight! I used to watch TV shows like *Hannah Montana*, and I used to sing every day in the car because I wanted to be just like her. That was my dream! And now *I'm living my dream*. You have to decide who your idol is and follow in their footsteps. You're not going to become them overnight, but with a lot of hard work and a lot of dedication—and patience—you can make that happen. Don't give up just because it doesn't happen in a week.

## Follow your heart.

If your heart is telling you something, listen up! Your heart doesn't lie. You have to trust yourself. You can listen to your parents and friends and other people who love you, but over the course of your life, you'll have to listen to yourself *a lot*. The more you believe in yourself, the easier it will be to follow your heart. No matter what, go for it! Dream big, believe in yourself, and be confident, Siwanatorz!

*xoxo,
JoJo*

# PeaceOutHaterz